T

Adopting a child

A
guide WITHDRAWN
for
people
interested
in
adoption

Published by
British Association for Adoption & Fostering
(BAAF)
Skyline House
200 Union Street
London SE1 0LX
www.baaf.org.uk

Charity registration 275689

© BAAF 1984, 1986, 1990, 1995, 1998
Sixth edition 2002

© BAAF 2002

British Library Cataloguing in Publication Data
A catalogue reference record for this book is available from the
British Library

ISBN 1 903699 06 1

Photography by John Birdsall; www.johnbirdsall.co.uk
All photographs posed by models
Designed by Andrew Haig & Associates
Typeset by Aldgate Press
Printed and bound by Aldgate Press

Contents

Acknowledgements

The first four editions of *Adopting A Child* were co-authored by Prue Chennells and Chris Hammond in 1984, 1986, 1990 and 1995. Jenifer Lord made considerable revisions for the fifth edition in 1998.

This edition draws on the previous editions but contains new material and significant amendments in light of recent government initiatives and legislative changes.

Our thanks go to the following people for all their suggestions and advice in the preparation of this edition including reading and commenting on the manuscript, rewriting sections or preparing new material, and preparing the text for production: Susanne Clarke, Marianne Harper, Marjorie Morrison, Alexandra Plumtree, Shaila Shah and Glynn Snow, from BAAF; Alyson Hurst from Adoption UK, Cherry Harnott from Portsmouth Social Services and Gill Haworth from Overseas Adoption Helpline.

Introduction

About 5,500 children were adopted in the year to March 2001 in the UK.* Almost two-thirds of these are children who have been looked after by a local authority. The others are predominantly children adopted by their parent and step-parent, and about 300 are children who have been brought from overseas and adopted by people living in the UK. There is a chapter in this book addressed to step-families considering adoption and one to people considering adopting from overseas. The rest of this book is about the adoption of children who are looked after by local authorities. There is also a chapter on meeting these children's needs through fostering.

There are currently about 66,700** children looked after by local authorities in the UK, two-thirds of them in foster homes. The vast majority, about 70 per cent, of the total number of looked after children will return home to their family within a year.

Although the number of looked after children who are adopted has risen in recent years, it still represents a tiny proportion, about 5 per cent, of all looked after children. Sixty per cent of the looked after children adopted recently in England were aged between one and four. In Scotland, too, this pre-school age group of children formed a significant percentage of children placed for adoption with 2 – 5-year-olds being the largest group. This reflects the wishes of many adopters to parent pre-school children and the relative ease with which adoption agencies are able to recruit adopters for young children. It doesn't reflect the needs of many waiting children for whom new families are urgently needed.

* Figures are estimated, based on information available from different parts of the UK. There are some variations in the detail of what is collected and the most recent figures available but efforts have been made to ensure that the overall picture is realistic.

** The figures used here exclude those children in Scotland who are "looked after" but who remain at home under supervision from the Children's Hearing system.

The majority of children who wait for adoption are aged five or above. There are single children and groups of brothers and sisters who need placement together and there are children with disabilities who range in age from babies upwards. There are children from a huge variety of ethnic, religious and cultural backgrounds, all of whom need families who match their backgrounds as closely as possible. Many of the children have been abused and/or neglected before they come into local authority care and they will have been further confused and upset by uncertainty and moves after coming into care.

Just as there is a wide range of children needing adoption, so will a wide range of people be welcomed by adoption agencies to adopt them. People of every ethnic, religious and cultural background, couples and single people – heterosexual as well as lesbian and gay, both with or without children – older people, people who have been divorced, all can and do become successful adoptive parents. And the great majority of adoptions work out well. Like all parents, adoptive parents get huge joy and satisfaction from parenting their children, as well as finding it very hard work and sometimes frustrating and painful.

Traditionally, adoption, for children not previously known to the families adopting them, was seen as severing connections with the past and starting afresh. Now we understand how important it is to provide adoptive parents with as much information as possible to pass on to their children, and how important their heritage is for those children. More and more of them, especially the older ones, are being adopted yet continue to maintain important relationships – sometimes with their birth parents, more often with other family members like brothers and sisters, grandparents, aunts and uncles.

Adoption agencies do not expect you to know all about adoption before you approach them. They will provide information and opportunities for you to find out about what will be involved, for instance, by introducing you to experienced adoptive parents. They are also working hard to provide better help and support to you and your child once you are living together and after you have adopted. Help is also available from adoptive parents' support groups and from post-adoption centres.

We hope that this book will answer most of your initial questions as well as clarify anything that may have previously puzzled you about adoption – the processes, the cost, the legal issues, etc. All these and many other issues are addressed in this book. These are illustrated with real life experiences in which people candidly talk about what went right and what went wrong and how they were helped or helped themselves create a safe, secure and loving family environment for a child or children who needed this. For children who have to be separated from their birth families, having a new permanent family by adoption is very much an experience that must fulfil *their* needs and help them through to a fulfilling adulthood.

A glossary of terms that are used in this book and which may be unfamiliar to you is provided at the end.

Changes in the law

Adoption Standards for the adoption work done in England were introduced by the Government in August 2001. The exceptions were Standards for intercountry adoption and adoption by step-parents but these are currently being worked on. Standards for adoption work in Wales are currently under discussion. National Care Standards covering adoption work in Scotland are nearing completion. Your local BAAF office or a local adoption agency will be able to give you up-to-date information and tell you where you can get a copy of the relevant standards. The good practice underpinned by the Standards forms the basis of this book.

At the time of going to press, a new Adoption and Children Bill for England and Wales was being debated in Parliament. This could be enacted by the summer of 2002 although it probably will not be implemented before 2004. Some of the possible changes include placement orders to take the place of freeing, an independent appeal system for prospective adopters who are turned down, the possibility of an unmarried couple being able to adopt jointly and a birth parent no longer needing to adopt with a step-parent. Reviews of the assessment of adopters, of the role of panels and of the provision of post-adoption support were also being undertaken in England.

In 2001, Scotland established an Adoption Policy Review Group. This has completed its first stage looking at areas of practice. The second stage planned for 2002 is to consider the need for legal changes.

It is expected that the UK will ratify the Hague Convention on intercountry adoption within the next year. This will provide for agreed arrangements for adoptions between Convention countries and for mutual recognition of adoption orders made in those countries.

Adoption is changing and developing and it will be important for you to check with BAAF and/or with a local adoption agency about any significant changes at the time you make your initial enquiries.

Scope of this edition

Almost all the content of this edition applies to the whole of the UK, although recognising that there are variations between different constitutent countries. Most of the text should also be useful in Northern Ireland.

Adoption as a legal process was first established in 1926 in England and Wales and in 1930 in Scotland. Although these are two separate jurisdictions, the legal framework for adoption was very similar and was primarily about legal security for babies relinquished by their birth parents. Now that most children placed for adoption with non relatives have spent a period looked after by the local authority, planning for them must also take account of other child care legislation. There is wider variation in this between Scotland and England and Wales especially given the particular position of the Children's Hearing system in Scotland. Devolution too is playing more of a part. The statutory basis for the service is first of all in the primary legislation and then in the regulations that provide more detail.

To date, legislation for England and Wales has been followed by one set of regulations. The new legislation referred to above will be followed by separate regulations for England and for Wales. Scotland will continue to have its own legislation and regulations for all aspects of adoption. Northern Ireland tends to look towards England and Wales in developing its legislation.

However, there are some differences in practice and procedures. In Northern Ireland there are still a number of babies who come into or are removed to care at a very early age and proceed to adoption once they have been "freed" for adoption. However, adoption as a route out of care for older children is not widely used although efforts are being made to develop this.

As stated previously, most of the text that follows will be relevant to any part of the UK but more information about local variations can be obtained from BAAF's regional centres (see Chapter 9). The legislation provides for children moving from one legal jurisdiction to another so that children can be linked with families across the UK.

Just as the law has been updated over the 70 plus years that adoption has been possible, so practice has changed tremendously. The rest of this book will tell you more about this. One aspect of this that affects the delivery of adoption services is the change in local government. At first, much of the adoption service was provided by voluntary adoption agencies. Now there are fewer such agencies and most children placed are the responsibility of their local authority Social Services or Social Work Departments which also act as adoption agencies to recruit and prepare adopters. A number of the recently established unitary Councils have been looking at different ways of delivering services. Social services may now be joined with education or housing services so that where reference is made to Social Services or Social Work Departments or Directors, you may need to check the precise names/designations locally. Although these terms are not accurate when applied to Northern Ireland, as described below, we have used them for the sake of simplicity.

In Northern Ireland, personal social services are provided by 11 Health and Social Services Trusts in turn commissioned by four Health and Social Services Boards. Unlike England and Wales and Scotland, social services are not under local authority control. A list of all agencies appears later on in this book.

Children needing adoption

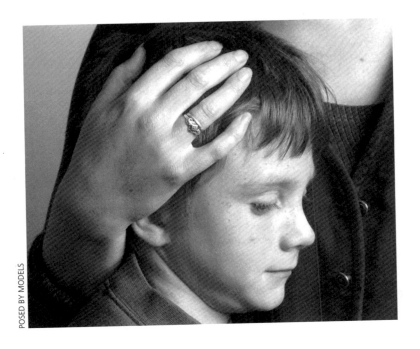

Sean and Simon are eight and nine and they've lived with us for two years. We adopted them nearly a year ago. We were totally exhausted for most of the first 18 months but we're starting to settle down now as a family and we have great fun together. The boys see their older sister, who's fostered, and also their grandmother, twice a year and that works well.

Probably at least 5,000 children currently in the care system in England, Scotland and Wales could be placed for adoption with families if the families were available. Although the children are very different, they all have one thing in common: a need for a family.

It is recognised that, for nearly all children, life in a family is best. A new family can bring love and security to the child – and a child can bring joy and satisfaction to the family. Every child is different and brings the potential for different sorts of satisfaction just as they will bring their own set of needs and challenges. The agency's job, with your help, is to match that child's potential and needs with your abilities and expectations.

Are there any babies needing adoption?

Of the 3,067 looked after children adopted in England in the year to March 2001, just 200 were babies under one. Proportionate figures for Scotland are similar – probably no more than 30 infants were adopted. Today it is easier for women to choose to parent on their own and fewer single mothers are placing their babies for adoption. Contraception is more efficient than it used to be, and fewer unplanned pregnancies occur. It is also easier to terminate pregnancies than previously.

There are more white people interested in adopting a white baby without disabilities than there are such babies needing adoption. Agencies have no difficulty in finding suitable adopters for white babies without disabilities and many already have quite a few prospective adopters approved and waiting to adopt. This means that people who want to adopt only such a child are likely to find it hard even to get started on the adoption road and most will not be able to adopt a baby.

By contrast, agencies are less successful at finding black families or those from other minority ethnic groups, although they are getting better at it. This means that if you and/or your partner is black or from a minority ethnic group, you are likely to find an agency to take up your application quite quickly. You will probably have a shorter wait before being linked with a baby although this will vary as only quite small numbers of black babies and those from other minority ethnic groups are placed for adoption each year. If you can consider slightly older children, your wait could be shorter.

There are some babies with disabilities or disabling conditions such as Down's Syndrome and cerebral palsy who need to be adopted. There are also some babies with genetic factors in their background, such as schizophrenia or Huntington's Chorea, for whom it is not always easy to find adoptive families.

Toddlers and pre-school children

Children aged between one and five are the largest group of children adopted in the UK. This reflects the wishes of many adopters to parent pre-school children and the relative ease with which adoption agencies are able to recruit adopters for young children. The majority of these placements work out extremely successfully. However, these children often have complex needs. They may have been abused and neglected and given little opportunity to make attachments to reliable parent figures. They may be very confused about all that has happened in their short lives and unable to trust in anyone. In addition, there may also be uncertainties about their development which may not be resolved until they are older. Families need to be able to take on these issues and to access support and advice.

What about older children?

The majority of children waiting to be adopted are aged five or over. Older children can benefit from family life. They may have lived for some years with one or both of their parents, or other family members, or they may have had many moves in and out of foster homes, and the damage done by these experiences can last a very long time. Older children need especially resilient parents who can help them face up to the past – including their possible need to keep in touch with some members of their family – and see them through the difficult adolescent years to maturity. In a loving and secure home, most of these children will eventually begin to thrive, although the older they are, the longer it may take.

Won't older children have a lot of problems?

Children who have been looked after by a local authority for months or years are likely to have emotional and behavioural problems because of the experiences which led to them having to be separated from their birth families, but also because of not having a permanent parent figure in their lives. Even young children soon learn that there isn't much point in getting attached to an adult who is soon going to disappear out of their lives. They may find it difficult to become attached to a new family and may act up or test out the new parents in an effort to get the attention they have been missing. Young children may be more like babies in their behaviour sometimes, and even teenagers may act like very young children. But most children of all ages can eventually settle down when they realise that they really are part of the family.

There are some children who have been so hurt by their past experiences that they will go on having special needs throughout their childhood, even though they have clearly benefited from becoming a loved member of the family. If you choose to adopt a

> **Donna came to us when she was nine. She was so moody – lovely one day, terrible the next. We often wondered if we'd make it to adoption! We kept telling each other about the reasons she was so difficult – she'd had a hard life, moved from place to place. We still have some bad patches, but nothing like we used to. We wouldn't be without her for the world.**

child who may have particular ongoing needs, you should ensure that the agency will make arrangements for them to have any special help they may continue to require on a long-term basis.

| **Groups of brothers and sisters**

Over half of all the children waiting for adoptive families are in groups of brothers and sisters needing to be placed together. Most of these children are in groups of two or three although there are some groups of four or more. Brothers and sisters can provide support and comfort for each other throughout their lives. If they want to stay together and if an assessment of their needs has shown that one family could parent them successfully, it is very sad if they have to be separated because no families come forward for them all. You may be daunted by the practicalities, but extra help and support could and should be available (see Chapter 4). Brothers and sisters share a family history and can support each other in making sense of what has happened to them. Research indicates that, compared to children of the same age placed on their own, brothers and sisters placed together are probably more likely to have a successful outcome.

> **I'm not married and I haven't any children of my own. When I discovered it was possible for single people to adopt, I went along to my local social work department and applied to take two school-age children. With three married brothers, all with children, I've had plenty of practice and I'm used to having children running around the house. The department took a bit of convincing but six months ago Vicky and her brother Tony joined me. Looking after two lively children of ten and eight is hard work and I'm glad that one of my brothers lives very close by. You do need help and support and someone to grumble at sometimes.**

| **Disabled children**

Disabled children may be placed for adoption at a very young age when their parents feel unable to care for them, or they may be looked after by the local authority after their parents have tried unsuccessfully to cope. So they may feel the impact both of their disability, the loss of their family of origin, and perhaps the confusion of a residential setting where different staff come and go. People who adopt these children will need to be prepared for a challenging yet rewarding task, as some of the children will never be able to lead entirely independent lives. In some cases, experience of disability in prospective adopters – either their own personal or professional experience or that of their children – will be positively welcomed (see *Whatever Happened to Adam?* in Further Reading).

Learning disabilities/difficulties

There are many babies and older children who have learning difficulties/disabilities waiting for adoption. For example, children with Down's Syndrome or foetal alcohol syndrome. These are children who, as well as individual love and care, need additional help and support to enable them to participate in as many as possible of the experiences and opportunities open to any other child.

> We've got three sons, and Danny, our youngest, was born with Down's Syndrome. When we saw the article in our local paper about four-year-old Annie needing a home it struck a chord at once; Annie's got Down's Syndrome too. Some people seemed to think it was odd that anyone would want a second child like that but we knew from experience how rewarding they can be – and we'd built up all that useful knowledge on schools and things for Danny already. Annie joined us nearly a year ago and we adopted her last month – the family wouldn't be the same without her.

There are many children whose learning disabilities are not clear-cut: they may have suffered an accident or injury while very young which has affected their ability to learn or to understand the world around them – but no-one knows how much. Or they may have been born with a disability that isn't clear to doctors. Sometimes they may be physically disabled too. Just like any other children they all need love and attention and the opportunity of family life and they all respond to it.

Physical disabilities

There are many types of physical disability – cerebral palsy, muscular dystrophy, spina bifida and cystic fibrosis are just some of them. Children with these disabilities need the love and security that life in a family offers just as much as other children. And, like most children, they will give love and affection in return. Having a physical disability does not mean having a learning disability too, although people sometimes confuse the two. People with physical disabilities can lead increasingly independent lives nowadays – especially if they have the support of a loving family.

Are both black and white children waiting to be adopted?

Yes, there are children from a great variety of ethnic, cultural and religious backgrounds waiting for adoption. They all need families who match their culture, "race", religion and language as closely as possible.

I'm from Jamaica and my husband is Scottish. We were shocked when we learnt how many children with one black and one white parent are in the care system. We've adopted Jamie, who is now four and we've just been matched with a little brother for him, who is two.

Do the children all have contact with their birth families?

It depends on what is meant by contact. It can mean anything from an adoption where the child has regular face-to-face contact with members of his or her birth family to an adoption where the adopters have met the birth parents once and there is an annual letter exchanged via the adoption agency. Many children being placed for adoption now will have a plan for their adoptive parents to have at least an annual exchange of news with their birth family via the adoption agency. Others will need and want to meet members of their birth family, sometimes grandparents, brothers and sisters, as well as their parents, perhaps twice a year.

Contact must be planned to meet the child's needs. These will change over time and everyone involved needs to be prepared to be flexible. Contact can often be very positive and can result in a child being more rather than less settled in their new family. Contact can sometimes be easier for everyone to manage if, as described above, the child's adopters match their heritage as closely as possible. You will need to be clear what the plan for contact is for any child whom you plan to adopt.

Who can adopt?

We can't have children of our own but we really wanted to be parents. After talking to a social worker in our local adoption agency we decided that we could consider school-age children. Abdul, aged six and his sister, Razia, aged four were placed with us just a few months after we were approved.

Are there long waiting lists for adopters?

No. It is estimated that at least 5,000 children looked after by local authorities in England, Scotland and Wales could be adopted if enough adopters came forward. They are children like those described in the previous chapter and adopters, both couples and single people, those with or without children already and people of various ages are urgently needed to offer them a chance of family life. The only group of children for whom there are more potential adopters than there are children, are white babies and toddlers without disabilities. Rather than keeping waiting lists of people wanting to adopt this group of children, agencies may have their lists closed. They then just recruit a few families as and when they need them for this small group of children.

Do I have to be "special" to adopt?

No, but understanding, energy, commitment, and the ability to face up to challenges and difficulties are all needed to care for an older child or a child with disabilities or a group of brothers and sisters. A good sense of humour helps too!

Just as you will be providing support and understanding to a child with a variety of different needs, so you will need support yourself. Your family, including your children if you have some, plus your close relatives and friends, need to be in agreement with your plan,

> We really wanted to adopt a young child, but we knew we'd have to be flexible. Our son, Alex, was only five months old when he came to us. His mother suffers from schizophrenia and his father may do as well and so we've accepted that Alex is more at risk than most people of developing a mental illness when he's older. We'll help and support him all we can should he become ill.

because you will almost certainly call on them for help. Your immediate family will, like yourself, be very closely affected. Children who have been hurt by their experiences can hurt others in their search for security. You will need all the help you can get. In return, though, you will get the joy and satisfaction of seeing some of the emotional damage to a child gradually start to heal. The rest of this chapter gives information on issues which you may be concerned or unsure about. The adoption agencies which you contact will also give you written information on their eligibility criteria for prospective adopters.

| Are there age limits?

You have to be at least 21 years old to adopt in law (unless you are a birth parent involved in a joint step-parent adoption, in which case the age is 18).

There is a greater health risk as people age. Agencies have a responsibility to ensure as far as possible that prospective adopters are likely to be fit and active at least until their child is a young adult. Some adopted adults record their feelings of discomfort at being placed as young children with older adoptive parents. Although there is no upper age limit, many agencies would not usually expect there to be more than about a 45-year age gap between the child and their adoptive parents. However, this is not inflexible and depends partly on what the adopters are offering in relation to the needs of waiting children. The average age of adopters in the UK is currently 38.

Birth mothers placing infants for adoption often ask for their child to be placed with parents within average childbearing ages. So, if agencies do take families on for babies for whom there is a huge choice of families, they may choose to work with slightly younger people.

| Do I have to be married?

No. Single people, both men and women, can and do adopt. If you wish to adopt jointly with a partner, the current law requires you to

be married. However, one partner in an unmarried couple –
heterosexual or lesbian or gay – can adopt. The other partner could
apply for a Residence Order. People who have been divorced can
adopt. If you are married or in a partnership, adoption agencies
usually prefer you to have been together for several years before
taking up an adoption application from you.

Do I have to be British?

No. You are eligible to adopt a child in the UK if your permanent
home is here (the legal term is "domicile"). In Scotland, you can
also adopt if you have lived in the UK for more than one year, even
if you do not have your permanent home here. In England and
Wales, you are not eligible for a full Adoption Order unless you are
domiciled in the UK. However, it is possible to obtain a court order
authorising you to take a child from the UK to your home country to
obtain a full Adoption Order there. You will need to be resident in
the UK for long enough to be assessed and approved as adopters, to
have a child placed with you and to apply for the court order
mentioned. This could take at least two years and possibly longer.

Most children needing adoption will already have had a number of
moves. They are likely to be insecure and to need as much stability
as possible. They may also have some ongoing contact with
members of their birth family. For these reasons it may not be
appropriate for many children to be placed with adopters who will
be moving around a lot or living overseas after the child's adoption.
It is important, too, for children to be placed with families who
match their culture, "race", religion and language as closely as
possible.

What if I'm British but working abroad for a few years?

Unless you are making arrangements for the adoption of a child
already well known to you, you will not be able to adopt a child in
the UK until you return to live here.

You need, for practical purposes, to be living in the UK for at least two years, so that the adoption agency has a chance to work with you and get to know you, and also to match you with a child and to introduce and place the child. This is followed by a period of at least three months, usually longer, before you can obtain an Adoption Order, ie. when parental responsibilities for the child are legally yours. It is not until this point that you will be able to take the child to live abroad with you.

What if I am disabled or in poor health?

Medical conditions or disability will not necessarily rule you out. All prospective adopters have to have a full medical examination done by their GP. The adoption agency employs a doctor who acts as a medical adviser. He or she may want your permission to contact consultants who have treated you. The adoption agency's prime concern is that you will have the health and vigour necessary to meet the needs of your child until he or she is a young adult.

There is evidence that smoking causes health problems for smokers and that passive smoking can damage the health of others, particularly young children. For this reason, many agencies will not usually place pre-school children with people who smoke.

Excessive alcohol consumption also leads to health problems. It may also be associated, for children in care, with violence and physical abuse. Your drinking habits will therefore need to be discussed with you.

There is also evidence that obesity can cause health problems as can anorexia or other eating disorders and so these conditions are carefully considered by the agency.

What if I've got a criminal record?

People with a record of offences against children or who are known to have harmed children cannot be considered by adoption agencies.

A criminal record of other offences need not rule you out. However, the nature of the offence and how long ago it was committed will have to be carefully considered. It is important to be open and honest with the adoption agency early on if you have a criminal record. The information will come to light when the police and other checks are done and any attempt at deception by you will be taken very seriously.

What about finances and housing?

You do not have to own your own home or to be wealthy. You may be eligible to receive an adoption allowance from the local authority in certain circumstances such as if the child whom you wish to adopt has special needs and if you could not afford to adopt him or her otherwise.

Does it matter if we're still having treatment for infertility?

You can certainly get written information from adoption agencies and also attend an information session or ask for an individual interview to find out about adoption. However, you will then need to decide whether to continue with infertility treatment or to pursue adoption. Adoption agencies will not usually be prepared to embark on a full adoption assessment and preparation with you while you are still actively involved in infertility treatment. It can be very difficult to pursue two different routes to parenting at the same time.

> **Doctors told us that there was no chance of us conceiving a second child. Our son, Mark, is now nine and very much wants a younger brother or even a sister! We saw Joshua in *Be My Parent*. He's only six but he's already been excluded from school once. His local authority are assessing us just for him. We're excited although we know he'll be a challenge for us.**

Experience shows that most people need to end treatment and "mourn" the birth child whom they are not going to have before moving on to think positively about all the issues involved in adoption.

> **We'd like to adopt a child the same age as our son so that they can grow up together**

There is quite a lot of research evidence which shows that it is much more likely that things will not work if a child joining a family is close in age to a child already there. Agencies, therefore, usually prefer to have an age difference of two years or more between children. It is also often easier for the new child if he or she can join your family as the youngest child. However, it is possible for children to come in as the eldest or as a middle child, so do discuss this with the adoption agency if you feel it might work in your family.

> **I'm white and I'd like to be considered for black children as well as white children**

The Guidance to the Children Act 1989 for England and Wales states that 'it may be taken as a guiding principle of good practice that, other things being equal and in the great majority of cases, placement with a family of similar ethnic origin and religion is most likely to meet a child's needs as fully as possible and to safeguard his or her welfare most effectively'.

The Guidance to the Children (Scotland) Act 1995 states that 'When considering the type of placement to be chosen, regard should be paid to a child's racial, religious, cultural and linguistic background. As far as possible, this background should be catered for within the placement, with carers ... sharing the child's religion and heritage. If possible, the location of the placement should not isolate the child from his or her community or cause him or her to experience prejudice.'

There are more white children than black children needing adoption and so it makes much more sense for white families to adopt white children whose particular needs they can meet as fully as possible. For instance, agencies would aim to place a child from an Irish Catholic background with Irish Catholic adopters rather than with an English family who are Baptists.

However much we may dislike it, we have to accept the fact that racism is still common in Britain today. So black children – including those of mixed (black and white) parentage who will be identified as black – will, sooner or later, have to cope with some form of racism. A black child who faces racist abuse outside the home will find it easier to discuss what has happened, understand it, and learn how to deal with it from a black adopter who can immediately relate to this experience. Coping with racism is something white people are not geared to, whereas for black adults it is a fact of life. Black children need this level of support in their daily life.

Black children also need black adults they can look up to. Images of black people on television, radio and in newspapers are often negative although this is changing. Black children need to have black adults with whom they can identify positively. For children who have been unable to stay with their own black families and who are then placed in white families, it can be hard to correct the false impression that white is better than black.

For black children and those from other minority ethnic groups, maintaining links with family members is important just as it would be for a white child. Matching heritage between a child and the adoptive family will make it easier for the child to settle, will help facilitate any continuing birth family contact, and will have the long-term advantage of the child learning about his or her heritage and culture.

However, sometimes a black family cannot be found within timescales which meet the needs of the child. In those instances where white families do adopt black children, they will need to ensure that their children can interact with members of their own community; if they live in a predominantly "white" area, the child will not be able to do this and may feel isolated and may be "singled out", for example, at school. Families will also need to enable the child to learn about and take pride in their cultural heritage as well as to prepare them for the problems they will face and explain to them that, although their parents detest racism, it still has to be faced in the world outside. This subject is tackled in greater detail in the companion book *Talking about Adoption to your Adopted child* (see Useful Reading).

I'm worried about an open adoption. Will this rule me out?

It depends what you mean by an open adoption. The term is used to mean anything from a one-off meeting with your child's birth parents and an annual exchange of news via the adoption agency to regular face-to-face contact between your child and members of their birth family. It is recognised now that it can be helpful for some children to maintain some face-to-face contact, perhaps with a grandparent or a brother or sister and sometimes with their birth parents. Face-to-face contact is not the plan for all children and you can discuss with the agency your wish not to have a child who needs this to be linked with you.

However, *all* adoptive parents need to have an open attitude to their child's birth family and past. You need to recognise the importance of this for your child and be prepared to talk with your child about his or her often confused feelings about their birth family and their past. You also have to accept that things can change and that your child *may* want direct contact in the future even though that isn't the plan now.

A one-off meeting with birth parents can be very valuable in helping you talk with your child about their birth family and it can be reassuring for the child to know that you have met his or her birth parents. Most adoption agencies would expect you to be prepared for a one-off meeting. They would also expect that you could consider at least an annual exchange of news, usually anonymously via the adoption agency, with your child's birth parents.

Can I adopt my foster child?

This is discussed in Chapter 7.

Can I adopt a member of my family?

The law in both England and Wales and in Scotland allows a child to be placed for adoption with his or her brother, sister, uncle, aunt or grandparent, without this needing to be agreed by an adoption agency.

For a child who is unable to live with his or her birth parents, living with a member of their extended family may well be the next best thing. However, there are other ways to give the child security which may be better than adoption. For instance, a Residence Order gives the carers parental responsibility without taking this away from the birth parents and cutting the child off from them legally, as an Adoption Order does. If you are considering adopting a family member, you may find it helpful to talk this through with a social worker from the local authority where you live, before you apply.

If you decide to go ahead with adoption, you can apply, once the child has settled with you, to a local Magistrates Court or a County Court which deals with adoption or in Scotland you would petition the Sheriff Court. You also need to notify your local authority Social Services or Social Work Department of your intention to adopt. Once the court has received your completed application form, it will require a local authority social worker to complete a comprehensive report for the court into the circumstances of the placement. This is called a Schedule 2 report in England and Wales and a section 22 report in Scotland and will involve interviews with you, the child and the child's parents, who will need to consent to the adoption. Medical reports and checks will need to done. Should the child's parents decide to withdraw their agreement at this stage, the court can consider dispensing with it, if there is compelling evidence to do so.

If a child in your family is being looked after by the local authority and seems unlikely to return to his or her parents and you would like to consider offering the child a permanent home, you should contact the child's social worker or local authority as soon as possible. They will welcome your interest.

How do I go about adopting a child?

We were a bit overwhelmed by the numbers of children featured in *Be My Parent*. However, the staff in *Be My Parent* were really helpful and the social worker from our local adoption agency helped us think about the sorts of children we could parent. We're now hoping to be approved for two children aged between four and eight.

| First steps

It can be helpful to do some reading about adoption as it is today and about the sorts of children needing families before you approach an adoption agency. This book is a good start and other useful books and leaflets are listed at the end.

Many people thinking about adoption also often find it invaluable to speak to experienced adopters. Adoption UK is a self-help group for adoptive and prospective adoptive parents before, during and after adoption. It has local groups throughout England, Scotland and Wales which you could join and whose members will be pleased to talk to you (see Useful Organisations).

| Contacting an agency

This important step is fully covered in Chapter 9, followed by a complete list of adoption agencies in England, Wales, Scotland and Northern Ireland.

Can I respond to children I see featured in a family-finding magazine before I contact a local agency?

Yes, you can. Social workers featuring children in *Be My Parent*, *Adoption Today*, local newspapers and other media are happy to hear from unapproved families. However, their priority is to place their child with a suitable family as soon as possible and so they will follow up approved families first. However, if you are within their geographical catchment area they may well decide to take up an application from you. This might be because you are the most suitable (or the only!) family who has responded to their child. It might also be because they think that you are offering a valuable resource to a child, even if they cannot place the child to whom you have responded with you.

The child's social worker might ask an agency local to you to do the assessment on their behalf, if you live at a distance. Alternatively, he or she might suggest that you contact a local agency, as there are other possibilities for the child whom they have featured. As discussed in Chapter 9, you need to think carefully about being assessed by an agency a long way away as it may be difficult for them to offer you adequate help and support once you have a child placed with you.

What will happen after I've contacted an agency?

Agencies work in slightly different ways. However, you will probably be sent written information initially. You may then be invited to an information meeting with other prospective adopters. If you are still interested, a social worker may then visit you at home or invite you to their office for an individual meeting. (Some agencies move straight to this individual meeting and do not have a group information session.) Adoption Standards for England give timescales for this part of the process. You should expect to receive written information within five working days of your enquiry and to be invited to a follow-up meeting within two months.

Making the application

You will often be invited to complete an application form at this stage. Agencies will have discussed the issues described in the previous chapter with you. They will also have described the children for whom they need families and they must prioritise applications that are more likely to meet the needs of waiting children. If they decide not to proceed, they should discuss the reasons for this with you and they should inform you in writing. However, if you and they do decide to proceed, they will get your permission to carry out checks with the police and other agencies and arrangements will be made for you to have a medical with your GP. You will also be asked to give the names of at least two personal referees, friends who know you well, and they will be interviewed.

| Preparation and training

Almost all adoption agencies will ask you to attend a series of group meetings, where you can meet other prospective adopters and can learn with them something of what adoption and being an adoptive parent is all about. Adopted adults, experienced adopters and birth parents whose children have been adopted often speak at these meetings. You will be given opportunities to think about the impact of an adopted child on your family, about how you may need to adapt your current lifestyle and about the support and help you will need.

| What is the assessment or | home study?

This is the process by which the adoption agency gets to know you and assesses your ability to parent an adopted child. It is also the process by which you learn about what will be involved in this parenting task and consider, in partnership with the social workers, whether you have the necessary skills and strengths. You will need to be open and honest with the social workers – they will get suspicious if they think you are too perfect! They need to know what your limitations are (everyone has some) so that they can make sure that suitable help and support are provided and so that they can match a child with you whose needs you can meet. There will be individual interviews with you as well as joint interviews with your partner, if you have one. Your own children, if you have any, will also be involved.

| What exactly are they | looking for?

Social workers are looking for people who are open and honest about their limitations as well as their strengths; people who are adaptable and flexible and willing to learn; people who enjoy children and are willing and able to put the child's needs first; people who know that every child, even a tiny baby, comes with a past and a birth family who are important; and people with "staying power" and a sense of humour.

The assessment report

A written report will be compiled, with your help. BAAF's Form F1 is the form most often used to collate this information. You should certainly read the report, apart from the medical information, checks and information from your personal referees (which remain confidential to the agency), and you should comment, in writing if necessary, on anything that you disagree with the social worker about or that you think should be added.

The adoption panel

The report is presented to the agency's adoption panel for their recommendation. This is a group of people, including social work professionals, a medical adviser, a councillor and independent members, who are people with knowledge of and an interest in adoption. These almost always include at least one adoptive parent and an adopted adult. The regulations about membership of panels are different in England and Wales from Scotland, but their purpose is the same: to consider prospective adopters and make a recommendation to the agency about whether they are approved or not.

In Scotland, prospective adopters must be invited to the panel, and many agencies elsewhere do invite prospective adopters too. This is now an expectation in the Adoption Standards for England.

The final decision

After the panel has made its recommendation, a senior officer in the agency makes a decision about whether or not to approve you as an adopter. In England and Wales, if the agency is proposing not to approve you, they must write to you first giving you their reasons and asking for your comments. In England, Wales and Scotland, the agency must write and tell you their decision, whether it is approval or non-approval. It should be unlikely for you to get to this stage and not be aware of any concerns about you from your social worker. Research indicates that 94 per cent of people who get to this stage in the process are approved as adopters.

How long will it all take?

This process, from your first enquiry to approval by the agency, should not usually take more than eight months. This is the timescale in the Adoption Standards for England. Proposed National Care Standards for Scotland suggest that this timescale may be 12 months in Scotland. The whole process is described more fully in BAAF's leaflet, *Understanding the Assessment Process* (see Useful Reading).

Do I have to pay the agency?

There is no charge for the home study, assessment and preparation if you are adopting a child who is in the UK. However, if you are asking an agency to do a home study so you can adopt a child from abroad, they will probably make a charge (see Chapter 6).

What happens after approval?

If you have been approved by a local authority, they will consider you carefully for their waiting children. They will usually want you to wait for one of their children for up to six months, with a further three months if they are a member of a local consortium of agencies, before responding to children featured in family-finding magazines by other agencies. You may want to check on this before deciding to work with them. If you are still waiting after this agreed period, the local authority will, with your agreement, refer you to the Adoption Register for England and Wales for active consideration for children referred to the Register.

If you have been approved by a voluntary adoption agency, they will help you to find a waiting child. They will encourage you to respond to children in *Be My Parent*, *Adoption Today* and other media and they will probably agree to refer you to the Adoption Register straightaway.

| How am I matched with a child?

Your agency may approach you to discuss a possible child or you may respond to a child whom you see featured as needing a new family. You will probably talk with your own social worker first and will then meet the child's social worker and also, perhaps, their foster carer. You will also be given written information about the child. It is important, in the excitement of hearing about a possible child at last, that you take time to consider the child's needs carefully and how you will be able to meet them. You may want to follow up particular issues with the social workers or the foster carers or with a doctor, or check whether the necessary services, eg. special schooling, are available in your area.

However, if everyone decides that you really do seem to be right for a particular child, the match will be taken to an adoption panel, usually the one in the child's local authority. Your Form F1, the child's Form E (a comprehensive report about the child, comparable to your Form F1 and which you should have read) and a report stating why you seem to be right for the child, will be presented to the panel. Your social worker and the child's social worker will attend and you may be invited to attend too. As with your approval as an adopter, it is a senior officer who makes the decision about the match, based on the recommendation of the panel.

| How long will it be before my | child comes to live with me?

Once a decision has been made about a match, the social workers will work out with you a plan for introducing you and the child to each other. Introductions may be daily for a week for a young baby, or rather more spaced out over a longer period for an older child. They do not usually last more than six to eight weeks though.

You should discuss any doubts or concerns that you may have with the social workers during this period. If you really do not feel that the match is right it is much better to say so at this stage rather than later.

What happens if I'm not approved?

If the agency has not been able to approve you, you should discuss with them fully the reasons why. They will have been disappointed not to be able to approve you and will have thought about this very carefully and so you may agree with them that perhaps adoption is not for you. In Scotland, Guidance states that 'agencies may find it helpful to establish a reconsideration procedure for adoptive applicants' and a number of agencies in Scotland do this. However, you can, if you wish, approach other adoption agencies and start again. Sometimes, people turned down by one agency are approved by another and go on to adopt successfully.

If you feel that the service that you have had from the agency has been poor you can, if you wish, make a formal complaint about this to the agency.

What happens after a child moves in?

We'd been to all the groups, talked to other people who'd adopted – we thought we could handle anything Andrew might do when he came to live with us. We just didn't expect him to do nothing! Not talk to us, not join in anything we did – it was a real effort for him just to sit and eat with us. He even packed a case and walked out on one occasion. We had (and needed!) a huge amount of help and support from our social worker and from our local adopters' support group and also from our church. Andrew had a lot of help too and gradually he started to relax and to begin to trust us. We still have our ups and downs and family life isn't quite what we expected, but we are a family now.

Your child or children moving in is only the beginning. Adjusting to a different way of life will take time and there will be difficult periods. You and your child may well need help and efforts are being made to ensure that this is available.

What help will be available?

It is important to talk to your social worker and to the social worker for your child, before the child moves in, about the help and support and special services which may be necessary. You should be clear what is available and, if appropriate, referrals should already have been made for specialist therapy or educational or health services which your child may need. This will be especially important if you are adopting an older child who may have experienced considerable trauma, or a child who has suffered from neglect or abuse. In such cases, access to appropriate help will be crucial.

Social workers from the adoption agency you dealt with will offer you all the help they can during the settling-in period, and until the adoption order. Adoption UK also offers invaluable support and help to adoptive families, and there are local groups throughout the UK.

Will there be any financial help?

You should be clear before the child moves in about any practical and financial support which can be given. Many local authorities pay a settling in grant, especially if you are adopting older children, which could be several hundred pounds, to cover your initial outlay on equipment such as beds and car seats. If you are adopting a group of brothers and sisters, it is possible for them to pay towards, for example, a larger car and for equipment such as a large washing machine. An adoption allowance may be available for certain children, a group of brothers and sisters for example, or a child with disabilitites or with serious behaviour difficulties. Adoption allowances are means tested but you should enquire about this if you think you need this help.

Will support be available after adoption?

Many adoption agencies now have "after adoption" or "post-adoption" workers. They keep in touch and offer the opportunity to talk over issues. They also often organise group events on subjects such as managing difficult behaviour or talking to children about adoption. They can also help you access specialist services which you and your child may need. Most of the UK is also served by After Adoption or Post-Adoption Centres, which exist to help familes at this stage. Adoption UK can also provide valuable support from other experienced adopters. Efforts are currently being made to try and improve services around the UK for adoptive families.

What about the birth family?

Birth parents whose children are adopted usually find this a hard and painful experience. Sometimes they have requested adoption, but often the decision has been made by others, sometimes very much against their own wishes. However, they are often still very important to their children and many of them are prepared to co-operate with the adopters and the agency in offering what they can to their child.

It is usually to the benefit of the child if the adopters can meet the birth parents at least once and continue to exchange basic information

> I was really upset at first when Chantelle said she wanted to find out more about her "real" mother. Somehow it felt as if she must be unhappy with us. She always knew she was adopted and we'd told her what we knew about her mother, but she said she wanted some of the gaps filled in. Anyway, I helped her to get in touch with the adoption agency in the end, and having all the extra information really seemed to help. In fact, it's brought us closer together talking it all through.

about the child. This is usually through the adoption agency which acts as a "letter box" for a letter perhaps once a year. It is now recognised that maintaining some level of contact can be of benefit to children as they grow up and helps the adopters answer questions about the birth parents, what they were like, where they are now, and so on. Ongoing contact will not be right in all cases and will need to be handled sensitively.

This is something you and your agency will be discussing right from the start, so that when you become an adoptive parent you will have a clear idea of what sort of contact is likely to be the most helpful for your child. When agencies talk about contact they do not necessarily mean face-to-face meetings – in fact many arrangements for contact involve keeping in touch through letters and are often through an intermediary such as the agency. Only some contact arrangements, at present, involve regular meetings or phone calls between the child and people from his or her past.

For some children visits may continue after adoption. This may be with birth parents or with grandparents and other significant adults or it may be with brothers and sisters who are living elsewhere, perhaps in other adoptive families. Older children may know where their relatives are living and want a family who can help them keep in contact. Again, this is something that you, the agency, and the child, if old enough, will need to discuss and agree on well before the adoption goes through to court. However, it is important to remember that the child's needs and wishes will change over time and you do need to be prepared to be flexible.

Why do children have to know they are adopted?

Many children who are adopted were old enough when placed to remember something of their past and so they obviously know about their adoption. However, all children have the right to know about their past. Increasingly, it has been acknowledged that an open rather than a secretive attitude is more helpful to the child. After all, there is always the danger that someone else will tell the child without any warning, or perhaps in a hostile way, for example, in a family row. Finding out like this can be a terrible shock to a child who may well wonder what else you have concealed from them.

Even older children may be very confused about what happened in the past. They may blame themselves for the things that went wrong in their birth family. So it is important to be honest and to discuss adoption quite naturally, right from the start.

From the age of 18 in England and Wales and 16 in Scotland, adopted children have the right to their original birth certificate if they want it – although their adoptive parents may already have given it to them.

Adoption means that the new parents must be prepared to be open with their child. Our book, *Talking about Adoption to your Adopted Child*, can help you with the kind of issues you will face (see Useful Reading). This is when the information collected by the adoption agency about the child's parents and early life, often in a life story book, will be needed. Children who are not given any facts sometimes have fantasies about their circumstances or history and may well believe the worst, so it is kinder and fairer to tell them the truth. This is not something that you do just once. Children need to go over their story again at different stages in their growing up, understanding a bit more each time.

What if adoption goes wrong?

Some adoptions do go wrong – like marriages, they do not always work. The first few weeks and months can produce problems that no-one anticipated so there is always a settling-in period of at least three months and usually considerably longer, before an Adoption Order is made. Of course, the social worker from the agency will keep in touch with you and will help and support you as much as possible. If you feel that things really are going wrong during this period, and that you cannot continue with the child, you owe it to yourself and to the child to tell the agency.

Once the adoption has been made legal, the child will be legally yours just as if you had given birth to him or her. The sources of help described above will be available. If the problems cannot be resolved, the Social Services or Social Work Department can take responsibility for the child again. However, the adoptive parents will remain the child's legal parents until and unless the child is adopted again by new parents.

What will happen to the child if things don't work out?

If the child does have to leave, he or she will go either to a foster family or possibly to a residential home. If it isn't possible to resolve the difficulties with you, another adoptive home may be found, but the difficulties that arose between you and the child will have to be understood to try and prevent the same thing happening again. Sometimes agencies arrange a meeting, called a disruption meeting, which enables everyone concerned to come together and reflect on events and what can be learned from them. Sometimes the problems arise when the child is much older, 16 plus, and like many teenagers, is having difficulty feeling at home in a family setting. The best solution then may be to support the child in an "independent" setting such as lodgings. He or she may well value having you around to advise and reassure him or her even if living together is too difficult at that point in their lives.

Could I try again?

You may feel you and the child were not right for one another, and that you could succeed with a different child. If the social worker agrees with you, you may get the chance to adopt again. After all, different children need different families and just as a second attempt may work for a child, so it may work for a family. You could apply to the same agency again or to a different one. You would need a further period of assessment and preparation and the adoption panel and the agency would need to consider whether or not to approve you again to adopt.

5

How is adoption made legal?

POSED BY MODELS

We seemed to wait ages for the day of the adoption hearing to come round – in the end it only seemed to take a few minutes! We all went home and celebrated – it was such an important day for us and the children.

When you adopt a child, you become the child's legal parent. The child usually takes your surname and can inherit from you just as if he or she was born to you. All responsibility for making decisions about the child and his or her future is transferred to the adopters. An adoption is not legal without an Adoption Order made by a court. Once an Order has been made it is irrevocable and cannot be overturned.

How do I get an Adoption Order?

You have to apply to court for an Adoption Order. You apply in England and Wales to your local Magistrates Court, to a County Court which deals with adoption (now a network of designated adoption centres), or to the High Court; in Scotland you lodge a petition in the Sheriff Court or the Court of Session; in Northern Ireland you apply to the County Court or to the High Court. Your adoption agency should be able to help you with the process and the court. You will need to obtain an application form from the court and complete and return it. If you are not adopting a child who is looked after by a local authority, you will also need to notify the Social Services or Social Work Department in your area of your intention to adopt. They will then have a duty to visit you and your child from time to time until the Adoption Order is granted.

How long does it take?

You can apply for an Adoption Order as soon as the child comes to live with you, but your application cannot be granted in court until the child has lived with you for at least three months. If your child is older or has special needs, you will probably want to wait longer and give yourselves a chance to settle down together properly before applying to court. You will need to discuss with your social worker when the right time would be to apply to court. If a baby comes to you soon after birth, the Order cannot be granted until the child is at least 19 weeks old. If you adopt a child from overseas, from a country whose Adoption Orders are not recognised by the UK, the period the child must live with you before an Order can be made is 12 months.

What happens before the court hearing?

When the court has received your application form, it will require a social worker from the local authority which placed your child with you, or from the one where you live if your child was not placed by a local authority, to prepare a report. This is called a Schedule 2 report in England and Wales and a section 22 or section 23 report in Scotland. It is a detailed report which includes information about your child and their birth family, about you and about the placement, both the reasons for it and also how it is going. In Scotland, an independent person appointed by the court called a curator *ad litem* will prepare a report. In England and Wales a Children's Guardian (formerly called a guardian *ad litem*) may be asked by the court to prepare a report if the adoption is not agreed by the birth parents. These workers will need to talk with you and your child, as well as with the birth parents.

What happens in court?

Adoption hearings are usually very short if the child's birth parents are in agreement, and in Scotland you may not need to go to court. You need not expect it to last more than half an hour, and you should be told at once whether the Adoption Order is granted. A report will have been prepared for the court which the Judge, Magistrates or Sheriff will consider. You will probably be asked some questions, and so will the child, if he or she is old enough. The Judge must consider the views of the child taking account of the child's age, understanding, etc. Also, in Scotland, any child of 12 or over is asked formally if he or she consents to the adoption. The only reason to dispense or do away with the child's consent is if he or she is incapable of consenting.

What if the birth parents don't agree?

If the birth parents do not agree, the adopters have to ask the court to over-ride their wishes. The court can only do this in appropriate circumstances, for instance, if it judges that the parents are unreasonably refusing to agree. Cases like this are known as "contested adoptions" and if you are involved in one you will almost certainly need legal help. You should be able to obtain help with the costs, either through public funding (formerly legal aid) or from the adoption agency, and it is worth finding out about this at an early stage.

Can't the adoption agency sort this out earlier?

Adoption agencies in England and Wales sometimes go to court for a "Freeing Order" for a child, either because the birth parents want to agree to adoption early, or because the agency wants to look for a family for the child against the parents' wishes. In Scotland, when an adoption agency has decided that adoption is in the best interests of a child, and has notified the birth parents of this, a freeing application will usually have to be made if the birth parents do not agree with the plan. Once the child has been "freed", the birth parents cannot stop an adoption going through.

Are there any other legal issues?

Yes, a few, but if, as is likely, you are adopting through an adoption agency, it will usually sort things out for you. You can only receive a child for adoption in this country if he or she is placed by a British adoption agency, unless the child is a close relative. Remember that any other private arrangement to adopt is *illegal*. Also, two people can only apply to adopt a child *jointly* if they are married. If you are not married, only one of you can apply to adopt and be named in the Adoption Order. The other partner could apply for a Residence Order.

Will my child get a new birth certificate when he or she is adopted?

Yes, your child will be issued with a new short certificate in your name which looks the same as other short birth certificates. If you wish, you can apply for a long "birth" certificate, which will give your names and your child's new name. It will have "Copy of an entry in the adoption register" printed on it.

Isn't going to court expensive?

There is a court fee which is currently £120 in the County Court or £30 in the Magistrates Court in England and Wales. In Scotland the fee at the Sheriff Court is £46. The local authority responsible for the child may be able to help you with part or all of this fee.

What about legal fees?

If the birth parents do not agree to the adoption and decide to oppose it in court, it may get so complicated that you need a solicitor and a barrister if in England and Wales, or an advocate in Scotland. This means legal costs can rise, in some cases, to several thousand pounds. But you may be able to claim public funding – it depends on your income – or the local authority responsible for the child will usually pay most, or all, of the legal costs involved.

What about costs after the adoption has gone through?

Unless an adoption allowance has been agreed, when the child is legally yours the financial responsibility is also yours – just as it would be if you had given birth to the child yourself.

Our boys were ten and eight when they came to live with us. We couldn't manage without an adoption allowance, which is paid by the local authority that had looked after the children.

What about adoption from abroad?

I know that there are older children needing adoption here, but I really, really wanted to adopt a baby. I had a home study done by my local social services department and then I managed to find my baby son through an agency in Guatemala. I'm lucky that my cousin is married to a Guatemalan man and he's going to be very important to my son as he grows up.

Some families are moved by the plight of children who have been the victims of war or natural disaster, or who have been abandoned in orphanages, and come forward to offer a home to such children. Others who may have been unsuccessful in adopting from the UK the type of child they feel able or want to parent, may also seek to adopt from another country. In a few cases, families may want to adopt a child who is a relative, and resides in another country.

Where can I get advice and help before deciding on this?

You can approach your local Social Services or Social Work Department. They will be pleased to have an opportunity to meet and talk with you before you make an application to adopt from abroad. There is also a helpline run by the Department of Health and another run independently by the Overseas Adoption Helpline which can give you information about adoption from particular countries and what may be required. Adoption UK will be able to talk to you about adoption generally and AFAA (Association of Families who have Adopted from Abroad) will be able to help you with some of the issues particular to adoption from abroad. Written information is available from all these agencies and from BAAF (see Useful Organisations and Useful Books). Many of the issues that you will need to consider are also relevant for adoption in the UK and are covered in Chapter 2.

Surely adoption overseas is the best plan for children living in large institutions?

It may be the best plan for some children in the short term. However, children have the right to remain in their own family, their own community and their own country, if at all possible, and countries overseas are working to this end. They need help from more affluent countries, and from individuals in those countries, to achieve this. In some countries, the "loss" of their children to overseas adoption has triggered the development of adoption services, and programmes to improve child care services have been launched, sometimes in collaboration with or funded by child care services from more "developed" countries.

As children grow up they may feel anger and sadness and a sense of loss at having been "rejected" not just by their birth family, but by their country of birth. It may be extremely difficult for them to establish any links with their birth family and with their past unless their adoptive parents have made great efforts to keep this alive for them.

If the child has been placed with adoptive parents of a different culture, "race", religion and language, they will also be disadvantaged in establishing a positive sense of identity and cultural heritage, and in coping with any racism which they will encounter. Special efforts will need to be made to help counter this.

Wouldn't countries in crisis welcome this sort of help?

In an emergency, it is impossible to gather the information needed to make a decision about whether the child really needs adoption. For example, are the child's parents alive or not? They may be in hospital, in prison, in hiding or refugees in another country, and may re-emerge to claim their child later. Intercountry adoption is not a suitable way of dealing with the needs of children who are moved as a result of war, famine, or other emergency. Indeed, many of these children will be emotionally damaged by abandonment, malnutrition, the effects of war, and separation from their families. In a crisis, the child needs to be made safe in as familiar an environment as possible. Experienced aid workers find

We adopted two children from El Salvador. Our son, Luis, isn't interested in his birth family, but our daughter, Alicia, is sad and angry that we have virtually no information about her first family. She blames us for this.

that the vast majority of children separated from their families by war or other emergency can be reunited with relatives when the crisis recedes. What is required is temporary care in a secure and loving environment, not the permanence of adoption.

I really only want a child without health problems

There can be no guarantee about this when you adopt from abroad. There is often very little information available about the child's early experiences and medical history or that of their birth parents, all of which will have implications for the child. Depending on the country of origin the child may have been exposed to the risk of conditions such as tuberculosis, HIV infection, Hepatitis B and C. Reliable and safe testing may not always be available. The child may also have suffered considerable physical, emotional and intellectual deprivation which may have long-term effects. Other factors, for example, the likelihood of any inherited conditions, will probably never be known until they manifest themselves.

Do I have to have a home study done?

Yes. You must have a home study done by the Social Services or Social Work Department for the area where you live or by an approved voluntary adoption agency which is also approved as an intercountry adoption agency. It is now *illegal* to commission a private home study report. The home study report is sent to the Department of Health, the Scottish Executive, the National Assembly for Wales or Northern Ireland Department of Health and

Our daughter, Amy, has a serious congenital hearing loss which we didn't know about when we adopted her from China. We love her and we are coping, although we'd always said that we didn't want to adopt a child with a disability.

the Overseas Adoption Helpline should be able to give you information on these.

I would like to adopt a child overseas who is related to me

If there has been a crisis in your extended family overseas and, for instance, a child's parents have died suddenly, you can apply for that child to join you in the UK as a dependent. You need to apply to the nearest British Diplomatic Post in the child's country. If it is agreed that the child has no other family locally able or willing to care and that the child needs to join you, entry clearance to the UK and indefinite leave to stay may be granted. Once the child has settled with you in the UK, you can decide whether or not adoption would be a good idea.

However, it may be that a relative overseas is planning to help you in your wish to be a parent by giving you one of their children, or you may wish to adopt a child in your extended family overseas who is living in poverty or difficult circumstances. The process in this situation would be to apply to an adoption agency here for a home study, as described earlier in this chapter, but to check out at the same time, through the British Diplomatic Post in the child's country and the Immigration Department of the Home Office here, whether entry clearance would be likely to be granted. It is unlikely that it would be granted for a child who is being "gifted" to you. Adoption has to be about meeting the needs of a child who is unable to live with their birth parents or other local relatives and who needs to be adopted.

What about fostering?

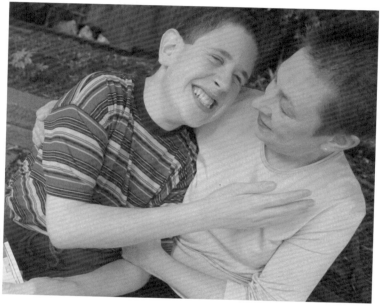

We've decided to apply for a Residence Order on Gareth and his local authority have agreed to pay us a Residence Order allowance. We've fostered him ever since he was nine – he's 13 now – and although he still sees his mother every month, there's no chance of them living together again, at least not till he's grown up. We'd like to be able to make more decisions about him. Gareth and his mum and his social worker agree. Gareth's part of our family now and that's all there is to it.

Fostering is a way of providing family life for someone else's child in your home. Most of the children looked after by local authorities when their own families are unable to care for them are placed in foster families. There are roughly 44,000 children in foster care in the UK, 65 per cent of all looked after children. Families are unable to care for their children for a variety of reasons. Sometimes parents have poor physical or mental health and have to be hospitalised, or they may abuse drugs or alcohol and need help to overcome their addiction. Children may have been neglected and they may also have been abused.

What about the foster child's parents?

Fostering is shared caring. Foster carers are not the child's legal parents and do not have parental responsibility. They usually share the caring with the child's birth parents, as well as with the local authority. Being a parent whose child is in foster care is painful, and foster carers need to understand this and to be sympathetic. Although they are not living with them, their parents are still very important to children who are fostered. Usually, they will want to see them often and parents will have a big part to play in making plans for the children's future, so foster carers and parents generally work closely together to do what is best for the children. Seventy per cent of children who are looked after return home within a year.

Children in foster care are often visited by their parents in the foster home. Foster carers must be prepared to help make these visits as easy as possible, in spite of all the uncertainties. Sometimes part of the task is helping the parent learn to care for the child. Other

We've fostered Stephen since he was 11. He still has regular contact with his birth family and he has never wanted to be adopted. We feel we're giving him a good start into independent adult living. We'll always be there for him, just as his birth family are.

relatives, like brothers or sisters or grandparents, may also keep in touch with the child, and foster carers need to encourage this.

Are there different kinds of fostering?

Yes. Some parents make private arrangements for their children to be looked after by private foster carers who are not approved and registered with the local authority. There are special regulations for private fostering (see Useful Reading). However, the majority of foster children are looked after by local authorities. These agencies work with parents to make plans for the children. Their parents may have asked for them to be looked after, or a court may have ordered that a local authority should share responsibility with their parents. In Scotland, a Children's Hearing may have made a supervision requirement, with a condition that the children reside with foster carers. Also, in Scotland, the court may have granted a Parental Responsibilities Order to the local authority giving them almost all parental responsibilities and rights and the local authority may have the child looked after by foster carers.

There are a number of specialist fostering schemes which your local authority or a neighbouring one may run. For example, some children need very temporary care, but on a regular basis, perhaps one or two weekends a month. This is often called respite care. Other children and young people need family care following a court appearance and this is often called remand fostering.

We just love having children around. We've got a grown up daughter and two teenagers at home and we also foster. We like having groups of brothers and sisters and we've got three at the moment. They're aged two, four and five and their social worker has just found adopters for them which is great, although we'll miss them!

| Could I foster a baby?

You can say which age children you would prefer to foster and, if you prefer to look after babies or small children, you should say so. But it is important to remember that fostering is not a way into adopting a baby or young child. You will be expected to care for the child short-term until he or she returns home or until other plans are made.

| Fostering and adoption

The vast majority of fostered children are able to return to their birth families. Many children need help for only a few days or weeks, but others may stay for months or even several years while permanent plans are made and carried out. For some children, adoption becomes the plan and foster carers have an important role in helping the child to move on to their new permanent family.

Fostering does not usually lead on to adoption. You have to get used to seeing a child leaving your home, a child you have grown to love. But it can be very satisfying – children who arrive frightened and upset can leave feeling much more confident. Helping a child move on is one of the most important tasks of foster carers.

Sometimes, however, there might be agreement between social services and yourself that it would be best for a particular child to remain with you or be adopted by you. This would need full and careful discussion and you would need to be re-assessed and approved as an adoptive parent. The Adoption Standards for England state that local authorities should aim to do this assessment within four months. Currently in England, just over 400 children a

> We've fostered a lot of children and have always felt very satisfied when we've been able to help them go back to their own family. This didn't work out for Anthony though, and when he was nine, and had been with us for nearly two years, it was agreed that he would stay with us permanently.

year, or 14 per cent of all the looked after children adopted, are adopted by their foster carers. A recent survey in Scotland found that almost a third of children needing a permanent new family found this by remaining with their foster carers, some through adoption and others through long-term fostering.

If you have fostered a child for a year or more and you want to adopt, it is possible to notify the local authority of your intention to adopt and to apply to court for an Adoption Order. However, it is much better to work with the local authority if you can. If you will need an adoption allowance, you will only be eligible if you work with the local authority.

Concurrent planning

This is the term given to a very small number of schemes currently operating. Children, usually babies or toddlers, for whom there is one last chance that they might return home to their birth family, are placed with families who will foster them with this aim. However, the foster carers are also approved as adopters and will keep the child, should the planned return home not be successful. In this way, the moves that a child may otherwise have to make are minimised. These schemes have to be run with the agreement of the local court and to tight timescales.

What about long-term fostering?

Sometimes, particularly for children aged 10 or over, foster care may be the plan until the child grows up. This long-term fostering cannot provide the same legal security as adoption for either the child or the foster family, but it may be the right plan for some children.

Some older children may accept, reluctantly, that they will never be able to return home to live and that they need a new family. However, they may be clear that they do not want to be adopted. They may also need a lot of extra help, for example, special schooling, hospital appointments, regular therapy sessions. You may decide that you would like to work in partnership with the local authority to offer long-term fostering to a child or young person. The child would remain the legal responsibility of the local authority and of their birth parents. For some children in Scotland, the local authority will have obtained a Parental Responsibilities Order, giving it almost all parental responsibilities and rights. You would receive a regular fostering allowance as well as being able to call on the local authority for help and support. You need to understand that most of the children for whom long-term fostering is the plan are at least nine or 10 years old.

What kind of people become foster carers?

Many different kinds of people are able to give children a loving and secure foster home. Some foster carers have young children of their own; some are older people whose children are now adults; others may not have any children of their own. Some people foster one child at a time, others more than one; some foster only babies or toddlers, others particularly like to look after teenagers. Foster carers come from all walks of life and live in all kinds of homes. It is the job of the social worker in the local authority or child care agency to find the right foster carers for each child, and this includes considering cultural and religious factors, among others.

Would I get paid?

Parents make their own arrangements about payment for private fostering, but when children are looked after by local authorities,

> I was a teacher of children with emotional difficulties and I first started fostering informally, caring for a couple of the children over the weekends during school holidays. Over the years I've cut down on the teaching and become a regular foster carer for my local authority. They tend to send me the older children with behaviour problems. I think they feel that I have the right background for it!

foster carers are paid an allowance. This allowance covers the cost of feeding, clothing and looking after the child. Fostering allowances vary from area to area and according to the age and needs of the child.

Sometimes, foster carers are paid more than just their allowances for looking after a child. They can be paid a fee in recognition of their particular skills and/or because the child whom they are fostering has special needs.

How would I go about fostering a child?

First of all, you need to contact your local authority. If you look up the name of your council or a neighbouring one in the phone book, the Social Services (England and Wales) or Social Work Department (Scotland) or Health and Social Services Board (Northern Ireland) should be listed; ask for the Fostering Officer. Social workers in local authorities often recruit foster carers through publicity in posters, leaflets and newspapers.

Voluntary organisations and independent fostering agencies can and do recruit, assess and prepare families for fostering. However, under current legislation in England and Wales, these organisations are not able to approve foster carers. In Scotland, voluntary organisations can approve carers, although ultimate responsibility for the child rests with the local authority.

Would I get training?

Many agencies run preparation and training groups for prospective foster carers as well as meeting with you individually. The whole family will need to be involved. If you have birth children, they will need a chance to think about what fostering will mean for them. Confidential enquiries will be made of your local authority and the police and you will probably be asked to have a medical examination. The local authority to which you have applied will consider a report on your application and decide whether you should be approved as a foster carer or not. This process usually takes several months.

| What support would I get?

The local authority must make a foster care agreement with you when you are approved. This covers expectations of both parties and includes the requirement, laid down in regulations, that you should not administer corporal punishment.

As a foster carer, you have to work closely with the child's social worker as well as with the child's birth family. In the early stages this will ensure that you know everything possible about the child, his or her likes and dislikes, normal routine, favourite foods and toys, etc. Later you will need to discuss the child's progress regularly with the worker and help plan for his or her future.

The local authority must keep records of foster children and foster carers. The local authority and foster carers must make a foster placement agreement, when a child is placed, about matters such as the arrangements for the child's health needs to be met, contact with the birth family and financial support for the child. The local authority must provide foster carers with written information about such things as the child's background, health, and mental and emotional development.

As well as having regular visits from the social workers for the children whom you are fostering, you will probably have your own social worker, who is there to support and help you in the fostering task. Foster carers should also be offered regular ongoing training.

| Residence Orders in
| Scotland

In Scotland, anyone, including foster carers, can apply for a Residence Order under section 11 of the Children (Scotland) Act 1995, if they can show that this is in the child's interests. A Residence Order gives the carers parental responsibilities and rights but not as many as an Adoption Order would and without removing all the birth parent's responsibilities and rights. A Residence Order lasts until the child is 16. The local authority can pay a residence allowance but is not obliged to do so. Your local social work department can tell you more about the orders.

Residence Orders in England and Wales and Northern Ireland

The making of a Residence Order under the Children Act 1989 or Children's (NI) Order 1995 gives people looking after a child more day-to-day rights than foster carers have, but not as many as adopters. The child is no longer looked after by the local authority but the birth parents are still legally involved. There are rules which limit the ability of foster carers to apply for a Residence Order if the child's parents or local authority are not in agreement. However, if a child has lived with someone for three years, that person can go to court and apply for a Residence Order, even if the local authority or parents disagree. The local authority can pay a Residence Order allowance, but is not obliged to do so. A Residence Order lasts until the child is 16 or, exceptionally, until he or she is 18. If you want to know more about Residence Orders you should talk to your local social services department or a solicitor with experience of child care law.

Step-children and adoption

POSED BY MODELS

When my husband and I divorced, Jordan was only one-and-a-half and continued to live with me. A few years later I remarried and David and I had Julia. We really wanted the four of us to be a family. David wanted to adopt Jordan but, after talking this through with Jordan, who still saw her father regularly, we realised that this would not be right for her. We are now thinking of applying for a Residence Order.

England and Wales

You are a stepfamily if you or your partner has a child from a previous relationship who is living with you. We estimate that there are as many as 2.5 million children in England and Wales living in stepfamilies at any one time. Only a tiny proportion of these children are adopted each year, about 1,700 children. However, these adoptions do account for about one-third of all adoptions in England and Wales (the others being looked after children and children adopted from abroad).

Most stepfamilies don't adopt. The adults involved work out satisfactory arrangements for the care and upbringing of the children, who will often have contact with the family members with whom they are not living. However, if you are considering adoption, the following information may be helpful. You may also find it helpful to read our leaflet *Stepchildren and Adoption* (see Useful Books and Leaflets).

Are there other ways to help make the child secure in our family?

You could apply for a Residence Order (see Chapter 7). This is a court order which sets out with whom the child is to reside (or live). It also gives the step-parent who acquires it "parental responsibility" for the child. However, it doesn't take parental responsibility away from anyone else who has it, eg. the child's mother or the non-resident father if the parents were married when the child was born or if he has acquired parental responsibility. In effect, the child would have three parents with responsibility for ensuring his or her welfare. You can apply for a Residence Order to your local Magistrates Court. It wouldn't prevent you applying for an Adoption Order at a later stage if you wish.

It is also important for the parent with whom the child is living to make a will, appointing a guardian for the child in the event of his or her death. If the step-parent is appointed and has a Residence

Order, the child will stay with him or her should their birth parent die.

We'd like the child to have the same surname as us

You don't have to adopt the child to achieve this. If the child's parents were married or the father has acquired parental responsibility, the child's surname cannot be changed without the agreement of the non-resident parent, unless a court gives permission. However, if the child's parents were not married and the father does not have parental responsibility, the child's surname can be changed with the agreement of his or her mother either by common usage or by a statutory declaration or by deed poll. You would need to consult a CAB or solicitor about this. Obviously your child's wishes should be taken into account. Many children now live in families where there are a number of different surnames and they may be quite happy with this and want to retain their own birth surname.

Does the child's other parent have to be contacted and to agree to Adoption or a Residence Order?

If the other parent is the mother, or is a father who was married to the child's mother or who has acquired parental responsibility, his or her agreement to adoption or to a Residence Order is necessary. A court considering an application can dispense with the parent's agreement but would need compelling reasons to do so. If the child's birth father was not married to the mother and does not have parental responsibility, his formal agreement is not necessary. However, the court would want to know what his views were and would usually require efforts to have been made to seek these. The court would consider the father's views in relation to the part he has played, or wished to play, in the child's life.

Does the child have to know what is happening?

Yes. The court will want to know what the child's views are. This would apply to children of five or so, and older. The court would want assurances that younger children will be told the truth about their parentage and about the adoption. This should usually start from when the child is about three, so that they grow up always having known.

Do we have to be married to adopt?

Yes, if you want equal rights and responsibilities in relation to the child. The Adoption Act 1976 specifies that only single people or married couples can adopt. If you are not married and the step-parent were to adopt, he or she would take over all the parental rights and responsibilities from the birth parent. To obtain equal rights and responsibilities you have to be married and to apply to adopt jointly. The fact that the birth parent has to adopt too is a reason why some stepfamilies decide not to adopt. You do not have to be married to apply jointly for a Residence Order.

What is the process for applying to adopt?

You must notify the Director of Social Services for the local authority where you live of your intention to adopt. It can be useful to arrange to speak to a social worker in Social Services to discuss whether adoption will be a good plan. If you decide to go ahead, you need to apply to a local Magistrates Court or to a County Court which hears adoptions. There will be a fee to pay. You will need to complete an application form. The court will then require a social worker in the local authority to complete a full report, called a Schedule 2 report, for the court hearing. This will involve interviews with you both, with your children and with the other parent. On the basis of this report, the court will decide whether or not to make an Adoption Order. This process need not take longer than three months, but can often take up to a year, depending on the circumstances of the case and the workload of the Social Services Department and the court.

Scotland

The situation is similar in that most stepfamilies do not adopt although these adoptions do account for about a half of all adoptions in Scotland. As in England and Wales, a Residence Order can be a good alternative and can give the child some security and the step-parent considerable responsibilities and rights. There are some differences in the law and in procedures in Scotland.

Change of name

There is a procedure whereby you can apply to change a name through the local Registrar's Office. You have to show that the child has been known by that name for at least two years. Your local Registrar's Office can help you with this.

Your child's views about adoption

The law requires that the child's own wishes and feelings are taken into account, as in England and Wales. However, in Scotland a child of 12 or over will be asked formally if she or he consents to the adoption.

Do I have to adopt my own child with my new partner?

No. In contrast to the law in England and Wales, a step-parent in Scotland is able to adopt the child on his or her own with the consent of the birth parent to whom he or she must be married.

Is the consent of the non-resident birth parent necessary?

Yes, if this is the mother or a father who has parental responsibilities and rights. If such a birth parent is in disagreement with the adoption, then the court can be asked to dispense with that agreement. There will need to be a proof hearing before the Sheriff. In this situation you would be well advised to use a solicitor.

What is the process for applying to adopt?

Petitions are usually lodged with the local Sheriff Court. You also have to notify the local authority where you live that you intend to apply for an Adoption Order.

When the court receives your application, it will appoint a curator *ad litem*, an independent person, who will meet with you and your child and prepare a report for the court. A social worker from your local authority will also visit you to discuss the application and will prepare a separate report for the court.

Finding an adoption agency

Unless you are a close relative of the child you want to adopt, you must apply to an adoption agency. There are nearly 250 adoption agencies in England, Scotland, Wales and Northern Ireland. Most of these are based in local authority Social Services Departments in England and Wales or Social Work Departments in Scotland. In Northern Ireland, social services are provided by Health and Social Services Trusts commissioned by four Health and Social Services Boards. These are listed in the following pages under the name of the county, borough or council, or Health Board.

There are also voluntary adoption agencies: Barnardo's is an example. Some of these are linked to churches, for example, the Catholic Children's Society.

Local authority adoption agencies covering large areas tend to take applications mainly from people within their area. However, agencies which are geographically small, eg. London boroughs, often prefer not to recruit adopters from their own area as they will tend to live too close to the birth families of the children who need placement.

Voluntary adoption agencies usually cover a wider area than the local authorities do, often covering several counties. So it is worth contacting voluntary adoption agencies in counties near to your own, as well as any in it.

You are not limited to your own immediate locality, but most agencies work roughly within a 50-mile radius of their office. It is important to remember that you and your child will need help and support from the agency after placement. It is much harder for an agency to give you adequate support if they are based a long way away and you should discuss what their plans are for this before you decide to work with them.

Would it be best to apply to the local authority or to a voluntary adoption agency?

Voluntary agencies tend to be small and to specialise in adoption and fostering work. They are often able to give very good support once a child is placed with you. Local authorities are bigger and have to respond to a wide range of needs. However, they are the agencies responsible for placing children and will consider families whom they have approved first. They may expect you to wait for up to six months after you are approved for the placement of a child looked after by them and for a further three months, if they are a member of a local group or consortium of agencies, for a placement through that group before responding to children from other local authorities whom you may see needing a new family. Voluntary agencies will actively help you to try and find a child, through using the Adoption Register for England and Wales, *Be My Parent* or *Adoption Today* and other contacts. So, there can be advantages and disadvantages in working with either type of agency.

What they are looking for

All the adoption agencies listed in the following pages are looking for permanent new families for school-age children, disabled children or those with learning disabilities or difficulties, and for groups of brothers and sisters. There are some black babies and toddlers who, like all other children, need parents of the same ethnicity as themselves. If you are white and would like to adopt a baby or toddler without disabilities you can contact agencies, but you must be prepared to find that lists may be closed.

British Association for Adoption & Fostering

British Association for Adoption & Fostering (BAAF) has close links with most of the adoption agencies listed in this book. You are welcome to contact us for advice about the adoption process and about finding an agency. However, we do not take up adoption applications ourselves. We have several regional and country offices in the UK, and we have included the address and telephone number of these on the following pages.

How to find an adoption agency

On the next few pages, you will find lists of local authority and voluntary agencies in England, Scotland, Wales and Northern Ireland. These are divided into five different groups; each of these is served by BAAF offices located in that area but currently there is no BAAF office in Northern Ireland – enquiries should go to the Southern Region office in London.

When you have found the name of one or more agencies that are reasonably near you, you can phone or write for further information. Agencies may also have a web site which you can visit. The Adoption Standards for England, which agencies are aiming towards and will have to implement by April 2003, state that you should expect to receive written information in response to your enquiry within five working days. You can contact a number of agencies at this early stage. However, you can make a firm application and enter into the preparation and assessment process with only one agency.

Unfortunately, we have not been able to include particular details about each of the agencies, for example, whether the agency occasionally needs families for white babies or whether it has a religious interest. A phone call to the agency will of course give you the necessary details. Your BAAF centre will also be able to help you. And a new web service launched by BAAF allows you to find some information about the agency – you can find this on *www.baaf.org.uk/agency_db/intro*.

ENGLAND: CENTRAL AND NORTHERN

BAAF REGIONAL CENTRES

Offices at:

St George's House
Coventry Road
Coleshill
BIRMINGHAM
B46 3EA
Tel: 01675 463998
Email: midlands@baaf.org.uk
Fax: 01675 465620

Grove Villa
82 Cardigan Road, Headingley
LEEDS
LS6 3BJ
Tel: 0113 274 4797
Email: leeds@baaf.org.uk
Fax: 0113 278 0492

and

MEA House
Ellison Place
NEWCASTLE UPON TYNE
NE1 8XS
Tel: 0191 261 6600
Email: newcastle@baaf.org.uk
Fax: 0191 232 2063

BAAF
North West

Jane Asquith
P O Box 96
WELLINGTON
Shropshire
TF6 6WA
Tel/Fax: 01952 771222
Email: north.west@baaf.org.uk

LOCAL AUTHORITY AGENCIES

BARNSLEY METROPOLITAN BOROUGH COUNCIL
Adoption and Fostering Unit
Wellington House, 36 Wellington Street
BARNSLEY
South Yorkshire
S70 1WA
Tel: 01226 775656

BIRMINGHAM CITY COUNCIL
Social Services Department
Louisa Ryland House
44 Newhall Street
BIRMINGHAM
B3 3PL
Tel: 0121 303 9944
www.birmingham.gov.uk

BLACKBURN WITH DARWEN COUNCIL
Social Services Department
Jubilee House
Jubilee Street
BLACKBURN
BB1 1ET
Tel: 01254 587862
www.blackburn.gov.uk

BLACKPOOL BOROUGH COUNCIL
Social Services Department
Progress House
Clifton Road
BLACKPOOL
FY4 4US
Tel: 01253 477649 / 477 656
www.blackpool.gov.uk

BOLTON METROPOLITAN BOROUGH COUNCIL
Social Services Department
The Woodlands
Manchester Road
BOLTON
Lancashire
BL3 2PQ
Tel: 01204 337480

BRADFORD SOCIAL SERVICES DEPARTMENT
Adoption & Fostering Unit
35 Saltaire Road
SHIPLEY
West Yorkshire
BD18 3HH
Tel: 01274 754331
www.bradfordadoptionfostering.co.uk

BURY, METROPOLITAN BOROUGH OF
Social Services Department
Family Placement Department
18 – 20 St Mary's Place

BURY
Lancashire
BL9 0DZ
Tel: 0161 253 5457
www.bury.gov.uk

CALDERDALE, METROPOLITAN BOROUGH OF
Family Placement Team
Ovenden Hall
Ovenden Road
HALIFAX
West Yorkshire
HX3 5QG
Tel: 01422 353279

CHESHIRE COUNTY COUNCIL
Social Services Department
Goldsmith House
Hamilton Place
CHESTER
CH1 1SE
Tel: 01244 603400

COVENTRY CITY COUNCIL SOCIAL SERVICES DEPARTMENT
Family Placement Service
Old Stoke House, Lloyd Crescent
Stoke Hill Estate
COVENTRY
CV2 5NY
Tel: 02476 659009

CUMBRIA COUNTY COUNCIL
Social Services Department
3 Victoria Place
CARLISLE
CA1 1EH
Tel: 01228 607138

DARLINGTON COUNCIL
Social Services Department
Fostering Team, Central House
Gladstone Street
DARLINGTON

Co Durham
DL3 6JX
Tel: 01325 346208
www.darlington.gov.uk

DERBY CITY COUNCIL

Social Services Department
2 Stanley Road
Alverston
DERBY
DE24 OEX
Tel: 01332 718000
Fax: 01332 718099

DERBYSHIRE COUNTY COUNCIL

Services Department -
Information Section
County Hall
MATLOCK
Derbyshire
DE4 3AG
Tel: 01629 585725
Email: gwen.rowe@derbyshire.gov.uk

DONCASTER METROPOLITAN BOROUGH COUNCIL

Children's Resources Department
PO Box 251
The Council House
College Road
DONCASTER
South Yorkshire
DN1 3DA
Tel: 01302 737845

DUDLEY METROPOLITAN BOROUGH COUNCIL

Social Services Department
Ednam House
1 St James's Road
DUDLEY
West Midlands
DY1 3JJ
Tel: 01384 815891
www.dudley.gov.uk

DURHAM COUNTY COUNCIL

Adoption Services Department
Aycliffe Young People's Centre
7 York Road
Copelaw
DURHAM
DL5 6UX
Tel: 0191 383 6023

EAST RIDING OF YORKSHIRE COUNCIL

Childcare Resources
31/31A Lairgate
BEVERLEY
HU17 8ET
Tel: 01482 887700

GATESHEAD METROPOLITAN BOROUGH COUNCIL

Family Placement Unit, Council Offices
Prince Consort Road
GATESHEAD
Tyne & Wear
NE8 4HJ
Tel: 0191 490 1616

HALTON BOROUGH COUNCIL

Grosvenor House
Halton Lea
RUNCORN
WA7 2ED
Tel: 01928 704359

HARTLEPOOL BOROUGH COUNCIL

Family Placement Team
Social Services Department
35 Avenue Road
HARTLEPOOL
Cleveland
TS24 8HD
Tel: 01429 523926

HEREFORDSHIRE COUNCIL
Adoption
Children's Resource Centre
Moor House
Widemarsh Common
HEREFORD
HR4 9NA
Tel: 01432 267 392
www.herefordshire.gov.uk

ISLE OF MAN
Social Services Division
MCAWS
3 Albany Lane
DOUGLAS
Isle of Man
IM2 3NS
Tel: 01624 625 161
Email: www.mcaws@ncb.net

**KINGSTON UPON HULL CITY
COUNCIL**
Social Services Department
Gleneagles Centre
East Car Road
HULL
HU8 9LB
Tel: 01482 799340

**KIRKLEES METROPOLITAN
COUNCIL**
Family Placement Unit
Westfields, Westfields Road
MIRFIELD
WF14 9PW
Tel: 01924 483707

**KNOWSLEY, METROPOLITAN
BOROUGH OF**
Social Services Department
Adoption and Fostering Services
Astley House, Astley Road
HUYTON
L36 8HY
Tel: 0151 443 3958

LANCASHIRE COUNTY COUNCIL
Social Services Headquarters
East Cliff County Offices
HQ PO Box 162
PRESTON
Lancashire
PR1 3EA
Tel: 01772 264362

LEEDS CITY COUNCIL
Social Services Department
Fostering and Adoption
3rd Floor West, Merrion House
110 Merrion Centre
LEEDS
LS2 8QB
Tel: 0113 247 4747

**LEICESTERSHIRE COUNTY
COUNCIL**
Social Services Department
Adoption Team
Eagle House
11 Friar Lane
LEICESTER
LE1 5RB
Tel: 0116 299 5917

**LINCOLNSHIRE COUNTY
COUNCIL**
Social Services Department
Wigford House
Brayford Wharf East
LINCOLN
LN5 7BH
Tel: 01522 552222
www.lincolnshire.gov.uk

CITY OF LIVERPOOL
Permanency and Adoption Team
Sefton Grange
Croxteth Drive
Aigburth
LIVERPOOL
L17 3EZ
Tel: 0151 233 1428

MANCHESTER CITY COUNCIL
Chorlton Social Services Office
102 Manchester Road
Chorlton
MANCHESTER
M21 9SZ
Tel: 0161 860 7666 or 0161 881 0911
www.manchester.gov.uk

MIDDLESBROUGH BOROUGH COUNCIL
Family Placement Team
Sandringham House
170A Overdale Road, Park End
MIDDLESBROUGH
TS3 7EA
Tel: 01642 300870

CITY OF NEWCASTLE UPON TYNE
Social Services Department
Fostering Unit
Shieldfield Centre
4 – 8 Clarence Walk, Shieldfield
NEWCASTLE UPON TYNE
NE2 1AL
Tel: 0191 278 8200
www.newcastle.gov.uk

NORTHAMPTONSHIRE SOCIAL SERVICES DEPARTMENT
Fostering & Adoption
John Dryden House
8 – 10 The Lakes
NORTHAMPTON
NN4 7DF
Tel: 01604 236172

NORTH EAST LINCOLNSHIRE COUNCIL
Adoption Service
2nd Floor, St James House
St James Square
GRIMSBY
DN31 1EP
Tel: 01472 325555

NORTH LINCOLNSHIRE COUNCIL
Social & Housing Services
Adoption & Fostering Team
38 West Street
SCAWBY
Near Brigg
North Lincs
DN20 9AN
Tel: 01652 656005

NORTH TYNESIDE COUNCIL
Children's Services
Camden House
Camden Street
NORTH SHIELDS
Tyne and Wear
NE30 1NW
Tel: 0191 200 5572

NORTHUMBERLAND COUNTY COUNCIL
Family Placement & Support Service
Tweed House, Hepscott Park
Stannington
MORPETH
Northumberland
NE61 6NF
Tel: 01670 534450
Email:
childservices@northumberland.gov.uk
www.northumberland.gov.uk

NORTH YORKSHIRE COUNTY COUNCIL
Social Services Department
County Hall
NORTHALLERTON
DL7 8DD
Tel: 01609 532608

NOTTINGHAM CITY COUNCIL
City Adoption Section
The Lindens
379 Woodborough Road
NOTTINGHAM
NG3 5GX
Tel: 0115 915 9332

OLDHAM, METROPOLITAN BOROUGH OF
Adoption Team
Marian Walker House
Frederick Street
Wherneth
OLDHAM
OL8 1SW
Tel: 0161 626 4947

REDCAR & CLEVELAND BOROUGH COUNCIL
Grosmont Resource Centre
20 Grosmont Close
REDCAR
Cleveland
TS10 4PJ
Tel: 01642 495910
Email:helga_cullum@redcar-cleveland.gov.uk

ROCHDALE METROPOLITAN BOROUGH COUNCIL
Family Placement Team
Foxholes House, Foxholes Road
ROCHDALE
Lancashire
OL12 0ED
Tel: 01706 710750

ROTHERHAM BOROUGH COUNCIL
SSCU
Family Care Unit, Brooklands
Doncaster Road
ROTHERHAM

South Yorkshire
S65 1NN
Tel: 01709 382121 Ext 6691

SALFORD SOCIAL SERVICES
Family Placement Section
Avon House
Avon Close, Little Hulton
MANCHESTER
M28 0LA
Tel: 0161 799 1762

SANDWELL METROPOLITAN BOROUGH COUNCIL
Home Finding Team
Hollies Family Centre
Coopers Lane, Smethwick
WARLEY
West Midlands
B67 7DW
Tel: 0121 569 5771

SEFTON, METROPOLITAN BOROUGH OF
Social Services Department
Connerley House
47 Balliol Road
Bootle
LIVERPOOL
L20 3AA
Tel: 0151 934 4580

SHEFFIELD SOCIAL SERVICES DIRECTORATE
Family Placement Service
Castle Market Buildings, 2nd Floor
Exchange Street
SHEFFIELD
S1 2AH
Tel: 0114 273 4950
Fax: 0114 273 4492
www.sheffield.gov.uk

SHROPSHIRE COUNTY COUNCIL
Social Services Department
Adoption Team
Observer House
Hollywell Street
Abbey Foregate
SHREWSBURY
SY2 6BL
Tel: 01743 241915

**SOLIHULL, METROPOLITAN
BOROUGH OF**
c/o Placement Team
Craig Croft Centre
8 Craig Croft
Chelmsley Wood
BIRMINGHAM
B37 7TR
Tel: 0121 788 4250

**SOUTH TYNESIDE,
METROPOLITAN BOROUGH OF**
Family Placements Section
Laygate Centre
38 Laygate Place
SOUTH SHIELDS
Tyne & Wear
NE33 5RT
Tel: 0191 424 4949
Email: family.placements@s-tyneside-mbc.gov.uk

**STAFFORDSHIRE COUNTY
COUNCIL**
Social Services Department
St Chads Place
STAFFORD
ST16 2LR
Tel: 01785 277033

**ST HELENS, METROPOLITAN
BOROUGH OF**
Adoption & Foster Care Services
73 Corporation Street
ST HELENS

Merseyside
WA10 1SX
Tel: 01744 456526

**STOCKPORT METROPOLITAN
BOROUGH COUNCIL**
Nugent Care Society
Children's Fieldwork Services
Blackbrook House
Blackbrook Road
ST HELENS
WA11 9RJ
Tel: 01744 605700
www.stockport.gov.uk

**STOCKTON-ON-TEES BOROUGH
COUNCIL**
Billingham Council Offices
Town Centre
BILLINGHAM
Stockton on Tees
Cleveland
TS23 2LW
Tel: 01642 397212
Email: child.placement@stockton.gov.uk
www.stockton-bc.gov.uk

**STOKE ON TRENT CITY
COUNCIL**
Family Placement Team
Heron Cross House, Grove Road
Fenton
STOKE ON TRENT
ST4 3AY
Tel: 01782 233745
www.stoke.gov.uk

CITY OF SUNDERLAND
Social Services for Looked After
Children
Penshaw House, Station Road
Penshaw
HOUGHTON-LE-SPRING
DH4 7LB
Tel: 0191 382 3108

TAMESIDE METROPOLITAN BOROUGH COUNCIL
Adoption & Permanency Team
West End Offices, William Street
ASHTON-UNDER-LYNE
Tameside
OL7 0BB
Tel: 0161 343 3339

TELFORD & WREKIN ADOPTION SERVICE
Observer House, Hollywell Street
Abbey Foregate
SHREWSBURY
SY2 6BL
Tel: 01743 241915

TRAFFORD METROPOLITAN BOROUGH COUNCIL
Social Services Department
Stretford Public Hall, Chester Road
STRETFORD
Manchester
M32 0LG
Tel: 0161 912 5050
Email: eileen.mcglone@trafford.gov.uk

CITY OF WAKEFIELD METROPOLITAN DISTRICT COUNCIL
Social Services Department
Family Placement Team
Flanshaw Children's Centre
6 Springfield Grange
WAKEFIELD
WF2 9QP
Tel: 01924 302160
www.wakefield.gov.uk

WALSALL METROPOLITAN BOROUGH COUNCIL
Family Placement Services
106 Essington Road, New Invention
WILLENHALL
West Midlands
WV12 5DT

Tel: 01922 710751
Fax: 01922 709719

WARRINGTON BOROUGH COUNCIL
Family Placement Team
Bewsey Old School, Lockton Lane
Bewsey
WARRINGTON
WA5 5BF
Tel: 01925 444283

WARWICKSHIRE COUNTY COUNCIL
Fostering Services
Farraday Hall
Lower Hill Morton Road
RUGBY
CV21 3TU
Tel: 01926 413313
www.warwickshire.gov.uk

WIGAN METROPOLITAN BOROUGH COUNCIL
Social Services Department
80 – 90 Ribble Road
Plattbridge
WIGAN
WN2 5EW
Tel: 01942 512068

WIRRAL, METROPOLITAN BOROUGH OF
Social Services
Conway Buildings, Conway Street
off Burlington Street
BIRKENHEAD
Merseyside
CH41 6LA
Tel: 0151 666 4653

WOLVERHAMPTON BOROUGH COUNCIL
Family Placement Service
Children's Services, Beldray Buildings
66 Mount Pleasant, Bilston

WOLVERHAMPTON
WV14 7PR
Tel: 01902 556556
www.wolverhampton.gov.uk

WORCESTERSHIRE COUNTY COUNCIL
Social Services Department
Children's Services
County Offices
Windsor Street
BROMSGROVE
B60 2BL
Tel: 01527 575855

YORK CITY COUNCIL
Community Services, Hollycroft
Wenlock Terrace, Fulford Road
YORK
YO10 4DU
Tel: 01904 613161

VOLUNTARY AGENCIES

ADOPTION MATTERS
14 Liverpool Road
CHESTER
CH2 1AE
Tel: 01244 390938
Fax: 01244 390 067
Email: info@adoptionmatters.org
www.adoptionmatters.org

BARNARDO'S MIDLANDS NEW FAMILIES
Owen House
Little Cornbow
HALESOWEN
West Midlands
B63 3AJ
Tel: 0121 550 4737
Fax: 0121 550 0967
Email:
midlands.newfamilies@barnardos.org.uk
www.barnardos.org.uk

BARNARDO'S NEW FAMILIES PROJECT
43 Briggate
Shipley
BRADFORD
West Yorkshire
BD17 7BP
Tel: 01274 532852
Fax: 0127 530998
www.barnardos.org.uk

BARNARDO'S NEWCASTLE NEW FAMILIES
North East Divisional Office
Orchard House
Fenwick Terrace
Jesmond
NEWCASTLE UPON TYNE
NE2 2JQ
Tel: 0191 281 5024
Fax: 0191 240 4801
www.barnardos.org.uk

BLACKBURN DIOCESAN ADOPTION AGENCY
St Mary's House
Cathedral Close
BLACKBURN
BB1 5AA
Tel: 01254 57759
Fax: 01254 670810
Email: adoption@bdaa.fsnet.co.uk

CATHOLIC CARE (DIOCESE OF LEEDS)
11 North Grange Road
Headingley
LEEDS
LS6 2BR
Tel: 0113 388 5400
Fax: 0113 388 5401
Email: adoption@catholic-care.org.uk

**CATHOLIC CARING SERVICES
TO CHILDREN & COMMUNITY
(LANCASTER)**
218 Tulketh Road
Ashton
PRESTON
Lancashire
PR2 1ES
Tel: 01772 732313
Fax: 01772 768726

**CATHOLIC CHILDREN'S
SOCIETY (NOTTINGHAMSHIRE)**
7 Colwick Road
West Bridgford
NOTTINGHAM
NG2 5FR
Tel: 0115 955 8811
Fax: 0115 955 8822
Email: enquiries@ccsnotts.co.uk
www.ccsnotts.co.uk

**CATHOLIC CHILDREN'S RESCUE
SOCIETY (DIOCESE OF
SALFORD) INC**
390 Parrs Wood Road
MANCHESTER
M20 5NA
Tel: 0161 445 7741
Fax: 0161 445 7769
Email: ccrs@lineone.net

**CATHOLIC CHILDREN'S
SOCIETY (DIOCESE OF
SHREWSBURY)**
St Paul's House
Farmfield Drive
Beechwood
PRENTON
Wirral
CH43 7ZT
Tel: 0151 652 1281
Fax: 0151 652 5002
Email: info@cathchildsoc.org.uk

CHILDREN'S SOCIETY
East Midlands Children's Resource
Team
Lacey Court
Charn Wood Road
Shepshed
LOUGHBOROUGH
Leicestershire
LH12 9QY
Tel: 01509 600306

**DONCASTER ADOPTION &
FAMILY WELFARE SOCIETY LTD**
Jubilee House, 1 Jubilee Road
Wheatley
DONCASTER
South Yorkshire
DN1 2UE
Tel: 01302 349909
Fax: 01302 340052
*Email: info@doncaster-adoption-
society.org.uk*

DURHAM FAMILY WELFARE
Agriculture House
Stonebridge
DURHAM
DH1 3RY
Tel: 0191 386 3719
Fax: 0191 386 4940
Email: durhamfw@compuserve.com
www.durhamfamilywelfare.org.uk

FATHER HUDSON'S SOCIETY
Coventry Road
Coleshill
BIRMINGHAM
B46 3EB
Tel: 01675 434020
Fax: 01675 434030
Email: socialworkers@frhudsons.org.uk

LDS FAMILY SERVICES (UK) LTD
399 Garretts Green Lane
Garretts Green
BIRMINGHAM
B33 0UH
Tel: 0121 785 4994
Fax: 0121 783 1888
Email: eng-lds-fs@ldschurch.org

MANCHESTER ADOPTION SOCIETY
47 Bury New Road
Sedgley Park
MANCHESTER
M25 9JY
Tel: 0161 773 0973
Fax: 0161 773 2802
Email: bc@manadopt.u-net.com
www.madadopt.u-net.com

MANX CHURCHES ADOPTION & WELFARE SOCIETY
3 Albany Lane
DOUGLAS, ISLE OF MAN
IM2 3NS
Tel: 01624 625 161
Fax: 01624 678304
Email: mcaws@mcb.net

NUGENT CARE SOCIETY
Children's Fieldwork Services
Blackbrook House
Blackbrook Road
St Helens
MERSEYSIDE
WA11 9RJ
Tel: 01744 605700
Fax: 01744 608065
Email: info@nugentcare.org
www.nugentcare.co.uk

NCH ADOPTION (MIDLANDS)
141 Wood End Lane
Erdington
BIRMINGHAM
B24 8BD
Tel: 0121 377 7999
Fax: 0121 377 7701
Email: mdap@mail.nch.org.uk
www.nch.org.uk

NCH FAMILY FINDERS (NORTH EAST)
11 Queen Square
LEEDS
LS2 8AJ
Tel: 0113 242 9631
Fax: 0113 245 8834
Email: Neape@mail.nch.org.uk
www.nch.org.uk

SOUTHWELL DIOCESAN COUNCIL FOR FAMILY CARE
Warren House
2 Pelham Court
Pelham Road
NOTTINGHAM
NG5 1AP
Tel: 0115 960 3010
Fax: 0115 960 8374
Email: admin@family-care.demon.co.uk
www.familycare-nottingham.org.uk

ENGLAND: SOUTHERN

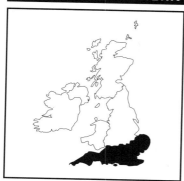

BAAF SOUTHERN REGION

Skyline House
200 Union Street
LONDON
SE1 0LX
Tel: 020 7593 2041/2
Fax: 020 7593 2091
Email: southern@baaf.org.uk
www.baaf.org.uk

LOCAL AUTHORITY AGENCIES

BARKING AND DAGENHAM, LONDON BOROUGH OF
Children & Families Division
Placement Services
512a Heathway
DAGENHAM
Essex
RM10 7SL
Tel: 020 8227 5818

BARNET, LONDON BOROUGH OF
Family Placement
34 Woodhouse Road
LONDON
N12 0RG
Tel: 020 8359 5701
Email: FPT.duty@barnet.gov.uk

BATH AND NORTH EAST SOMERSET
Social and Housing Services
7 North Parade Buildings
BATH
BA1 1NY
Tel: 01225 477930
Email: liz.price@bathnes.gov.uk

BEDFORDSHIRE COUNTY COUNCIL
Social Services Department
Houghton Lodge, Houghton Close
off Oliver Street
AMPTHILL
Beds
MK45 2TG
Tel: 01525 840543

BEXLEY COUNCIL
Social Services Department
Howlbury Centre
Slade Green Road
ERITH

Kent
DA8 2HX
Tel: 0208 303 7777 Ext 3829/3830
Email: adoption&fostering@bexley.gov.uk

BOURNEMOUTH BOROUGH COUNCIL
Social Services Directorate
Maxwell Road Depot
Maxwell Road
Winton
BOURNEMOUTH
BH9 1DL
Tel: 01202 535909

BRACKNELL FOREST BOROUGH COUNCIL
Time Square
Market Street
BRACKNELL
Berks
RG12 1JD
Tel: 01344 351534

BRENT, LONDON BOROUGH OF
Brent Family Placements Services
Triangle House
328 – 330 High Road
WEMBLEY
HA9 6AZ
Tel: 020 8937 1234

BRIGHTON AND HOVE COUNCIL
Social Care & Health
253 Preston Road
BRIGHTON
BN1 6SE
Tel: 01273 295 4444

BRISTOL CITY COUNCIL
Social Services Department
PO Box 30, Amelia Court
Pipe Lane
BRISTOL
BS99 7NB

Tel: 0117 903 7782
www.bristol-city.gov.uk

BROMLEY, LONDON BOROUGH OF
Social Services Department
Joseph Lancaster Hall
Civic Centre
Rafford Way
BROMLEY
Kent
BR1 3UH
Tel: 020 8464 3333
www.bromley.gov.uk

BUCKINGHAMSHIRE COUNTY COUNCIL
Social Services Department
Council Offices
King George V Road
AMERSHAM
Bucks
HP6 5BN
Tel: 01494 729000

CAMBRIDGESHIRE COUNTY COUNCIL
Homefinders Centre
Buttsgrove Centre
38 Buttsgrove Way
HUNTINGDON
Cambridgeshire
PE29 1LY
Tel: 01480 376404

CAMDEN, LONDON BOROUGH OF
Permanent Placements Team
Gospel Oak Office
115 Wellesley Road
LONDON
NW5 4PA
Tel: 020 7974 6164/5
Email: permanentplacementteam@
camden.gov.uk
www.camden.gov.uk

CITY OF LONDON
Social Services Department
Milton Court, Moor Lane
LONDON
EC2Y 9BL
Tel: 020 7332 1218
www.cityoflondon.gov.uk

CORNWALL COUNTY COUNCIL
Adoption & Family Finding Unit
13 Treyew Road
TRURO
TR1 2BY
Tel: 01872 270251

CROYDON, LONDON BOROUGH OF
Family Placement Unit
130 Brighton Road
PURLEY
Surrey
CR8 4HA
Tel: 020 8660 4844
Email: family-finders@croydon.gov.uk
www.croydon.gov.uk

DEVON COUNTY COUNCIL
Adoption Unit, Social Services
Foxhole
DARTINGTON
TQ9 6EB
Tel: 01392 386644

DORSET COUNTY COUNCIL
Fostering & Adoption Unit
Acland Road
DORCHESTER
Dorset
DT1 1SA
Tel: 01305 251414

EALING, LONDON BOROUGH OF
Fostering and Adoption Connections
Acton Town Hall
Winchester Street
Acton

LONDON
W3 6NE
Tel: 020 8832 6088

EAST SUSSEX COUNTY COUNCIL
Social Services Department
Children & Families Division
PO Box 5, County Hall
LEWES
East Sussex
BN7 1SW
Tel: 01273 481233

ENFIELD, LONDON BOROUGH OF
Social Services Department
Southgate Town Hall
Green Lanes
Palmers Green
LONDON
N13 4XD
Tel: 020 8379 2882

ESSEX COUNTY COUNCIL
Social Services Department
PO Box 297
County Hall
CHELMSFORD
CM1 1YS
Tel: 0800 801530

GLOUCESTERSHIRE COUNTY COUNCIL
Social Services Department
Bearland Wing
Sheril Hall
GLOUCESTER
GL1 2TR
Switchboard: 01452 425000
Direct Tel: 01452 427778

GREENWICH, LONDON BOROUGH OF
Adoption Team
147 Powis Street
LONDON
SE18 6JL

Tel: 020 8921 2752
Email: greenadopt@compuserve.com

GUERNSEY, STATES OF
Children Board, Homefinding Unit
Garden Hill Resource Centre
Swissville, Rohais
GUERNSEY
GY1 1FB
Tel: 01481 713230

HACKNEY, LONDON BOROUGH OF
Social Services Department
Adoption & Fostering
161 City Road
LONDON
EC1V 1NR
Tel: 020 8356 6350

HAMMERSMITH & FULHAM, LONDON BOROUGH OF
Family Placement Unit
2nd Floor, Barclay House
Effie Road
LONDON
SW6 1EN
Tel: 020 8748 3020

HAMPSHIRE COUNTY COUNCIL
Social Services Department
Trafalgar House
The Castle
WINCHESTER
SO23 8UQ
Tel: 01962 847176

HARINGEY, LONDON BOROUGH OF
Adoption Section
Grosvenor House
27 The Broadway
Crouch End
LONDON
N8 8DU
Tel: 020 8489 1481

HARROW, LONDON BOROUGH OF
Family Placement Team
Social Services Department
429 – 433 Pinner Road
NORTH HARROW
HA1 4HN
Tel: 020 8863 5544

HAVERING, LONDON BOROUGH OF
Family Placement Team
Midland House
109 – 113 Victoria Road
ROMFORD
RM1 2LX
Tel: 01708 434543

HERTFORDSHIRE COUNTY COUNCIL
Adoption Team
Old Parkway School
Parkway Gardens, Parkway
WELWYN GARDEN CITY
Hertfordshire
AL8 6JD
Tel: 01707 897654

HILLINGDON, LONDON BOROUGH OF
Fostering & Adoption Service
855 Uxbridge Road
HAYES
Middlesex
UB4 8HZ
Tel: 01895 277845

HOUNSLOW, LONDON BOROUGH OF
Family Placement Section
Social Services Department
26 Glenhurst Road
BRENTFORD
TW8 9BX
Tel: 020 8583 3447

ISLE OF WIGHT COUNTY COUNCIL
Family Placement Team
Social Services Centre (Ryde)
Town Hall
Lind Street
RYDE
Isle of Wight
PO33 2NQ
Tel: 01983 566011

ISLINGTON, LONDON BOROUGH OF
Family Placement Unit
292 Essex Road
LONDON
N1 3AZ
Tel: 020 7527 2000

JERSEY, STATES OF
Children's Service
Maison Le Pape
The Parade, St Helier
JERSEY
JE2 3PU
Tel: 01534 623500

KENSINGTON & CHELSEA, ROYAL BOROUGH OF
Family Placement Unit
Westway Information Centre
140 Ladbroke Grove
North Kensington
LONDON
W10 5ND
Tel: 020 7598 4499
www.rbkc.gov.uk

KENT COUNTY COUNCIL
Social Services Department
Fostering & Adoption
1st Floor
17 Kings Hill Avenue
Kings Hill
WEST MALLING

Kent
ME19 4UL
Tel: 01732 525000

KINGSTON UPON THAMES, ROYAL BOROUGH OF
Community Services Department
Family Placement Team
Guildhall 1
High Street
KINGSTON UPON THAMES
Surrey
KT1 1EU
Tel: 020 8547 6042
www.kingston.gov.uk

LAMBETH, LONDON BOROUGH OF
Adoption Team
Mary Seacole House
91 Clapham High Street
LONDON
SW4 7TF
Tel: 020 7926 8503

LEWISHAM, LONDON BOROUGH OF
Social Services Department
Adoption Team
St Paul's House
125 Deptford High Street
LONDON
SE8 4NS
Tel: 020 8314 6000

LUTON COUNCIL
Social Services Department
Adoption Team
Unity House
111 Stuart Street
LUTON
LU1 5NP
Tel: 01582 547600

MEDWAY COUNCIL
Social Services
Adoption Team
Compass Centre
Chatham Maritime
CHATHAM
ME4 4YH
Tel: 01634 331296

MERTON, LONDON BOROUGH OF
Children's Division
Family Placement Services
Worsfold House
Church Road
MITCHAM
Surrey
CR4 3BE
Tel: 020 8545 4277

MILTON KEYNES COUNCIL
Learning and Development Directorate
Children's Services
Saxon Court
502 Avebury Boulevard
MILTON KEYNES
MK9 3HS
Tel: 01908 691691

NEWHAM, LONDON BOROUGH OF
Social Services Department
46 Clova Road
Forest Gate
LONDON
E7 9AH
Tel: 020 8430 2000 Ext 45727

NORFOLK COUNTY COUNCIL
Adoption & Family Finding Unit
3 Unthank Road
NORWICH
NR2 2PA
Tel: 01603 617796
Email: adoption.unit.soc@norfolk.gov.uk

NORTH SOMERSET DISTRICT COUNCIL
Social Services Department
Family Placement Team
PO Box 195
Town Hall
WESTON-SUPER-MARE
BS23 1UF
Tel: 01275 888236
www.n-somerset.gov.uk

OXFORDSHIRE COUNTY COUNCIL
Social Services Department
Family Placement Team
The City Office
134B Cowley Road
OXFORD
OX4 1JH
Tel: 01865 815237

PETERBOROUGH CITY COUNCIL
Adoption & Fostering Unit
Suite 6
Staniland Court
Staniland Way
PETERBOROUGH
PE4 6NJ
Tel: 01733 746179
www.peterborough.gov.uk

PLYMOUTH CITY COUNCIL
Family Placement Service
Midland House
City of Plymouth
PLYMOUTH
PL1 2AA
Tel: 01752 306800

POOLE BOROUGH COUNCIL
Adoption & Fostering Team
Children & Families Services
14A Commercial Road
Parkstone

POOLE
BH14 OJW
Tel: 01202 735046
www.poole.gov.uk

PORTSMOUTH CITY COUNCIL
Social Services Department
1st floor
Civic Offices
Guildhall Square
PORTSMOUTH
PO1 2EP
Tel: 023 9284 1626

READING BOROUGH COUNCIL
Fostering & Adoption Team
Social Services Department
Reading Borough Council
PO Box 2624
READING
RG1 7WB
Tel: 0118 955 3740
www.reading.gov.uk

REDBRIDGE, LONDON BOROUGH OF
Fostering & Adoption Service
235 Grove Road
CHADWELL HEATH
Essex
RM6 4XD
Tel: 020 8708 7761
www.redbridgekids.org.uk

RICHMOND UPON THAMES, LONDON BOROUGH OF
Fostering & Adoption Services
Services for Children and Families
42 York Street
TWICKENHAM
TW1 3BW
Tel: 020 8891 7754

SLOUGH BOROUGH COUNCIL
Social Services Department
Family Placement Service
Town Hall
Bath Road
SLOUGH
SL1 3UQ
Tel: 01753 690 960

SOMERSET COUNTY COUNCIL
Social Services Department
County Hall
TAUNTON
Somerset
TA1 4DY
Tel: 01823 355130

SOUTH GLOUCESTERSHIRE COUNCIL
Social Services Department
Heath Resource Centre
2A Newton Road
Cadbury Heath
BRISTOL
BS30 8EZ
Tel: 01454 866 088

SOUTHAMPTON CITY COUNCIL
Social Services Department
Family Placement Team
315 Coxford Road
Lordswood
SOUTHAMPTON
SO16 5LH
Tel: 023 8079 9110

SOUTHEND COUNCIL
Family Finders
283 London Road
WESTCLIFF ON SEA
SS0 7BX
Tel: 01702 354366

SOUTHWARK, LONDON BOROUGH OF
Adoption & Fostering Unit
47b East Dulwich Road

LONDON
SE22 9BZ
Tel: 020 7525 4409

SUFFOLK COUNTY COUNCIL
Social Services Department
Adoption & Long-term Fostering Team
214B Sidegate Lane
IPSWICH
IP4 3DH
Tel: 01473 588536

SURREY COUNTY COUNCIL
County Permanency Team
Belair House
Chertsey Boulevard
Hanworth Lane
CHERTSEY
Surrey
KT16 9JX
Tel: 01932 566272
Email: familyfinding@surreycc.gov.uk
www.surreycc.gov.uk

SUTTON, LONDON BOROUGH OF
Adoption & Fostering Team
The Lodge
Honeywood Walk
CARSHALTON
Surrey
SM5 3NX
Tel: 020 8770 4799

SWINDON BOROUGH COUNCIL
Housing & Social Services
Family Placement Team
Hut 8
Civic Offices
Euclid Street
SWINDON
SN1 2JH
Tel: 01793 465700
Email: familyplacement@swindon.gov.uk
www.swindon.gov.uk

THURROCK COUNCIL
Families Placement Team
PO Box 140
Civic Offices
New Road
GRAYS
Essex
RM17 6TJ
Tel: 01375 652617

TORBAY BOROUGH COUNCIL
Family Placement Team
Parkfield House
38 Esplanade Road
PAIGNTON
Devon
TQ3 2NH
Tel: 01803 208181

TOWER HAMLETS, LONDON BOROUGH OF
Social Services
Family Placement Service
62 Roman Road
Bethnal Green
LONDON
E2 0QJ
Tel: 020 7364 2026

WALTHAM FOREST, LONDON BOROUGH OF
Social Services Department
Fostering & Adoption Assessment Team
6/8 Oliver Road
Leyton
LONDON
E10 5JY
Tel: 020 8496 2479
www.walthamforest.gov.uk

WANDSWORTH, LONDON BOROUGH OF
Adoption & Fostering Unit
Welbeck House
4th floor
43 – 51 Wandsworth High Street
LONDON
SW18 2PU
Tel: 020 8871 6666

WEST BERKSHIRE COUNCIL
Family Placement Team
Pelican House
9 – 15 West Street
NEWBURY
RGF14 1PL
Tel: 01635 516820

WEST SUSSEX COUNTY COUNCIL
Social Services Department
Adoption Team
Harwood House
Kings Road
HORSHAM
RH13 1PR
Tel: 01403 246416

CITY OF WESTMINSTER
Family Placements Service
33 Tachbrook Street
LONDON
SW1V 2JR
Tel: 020 7641 2848

WILTSHIRE COUNTY COUNCIL
Children's Resource Centre
357 Hungerdown Lane
CHIPPENHAM
Wiltshire
SN14 0UY
Tel: 01249 444321

WINDSOR AND MAIDENHEAD, ROYAL BOROUGH OF
Fostering & Adoption Services
Social Services

4 Marlow Road
MAIDENHEAD
Berkshire
SL6 7YR
Tel: 01628 683201
Email: adoption&fostering@rbwm.gov.uk

WOKINGHAM DISTRICT COUNCIL
Dept of Community Services & Housing
Family Placement Team
Wellington House
Wellington Road
WOKINGHAM
RG40 2QB
Tel: 0118 974 6877

VOLUNTARY AGENCIES

ADOPT ANGLIA PROJECT
9 Petersfield
CAMBRIDGE
CB1 1BB
Tel: 01223 357397
Fax: 01223 576602

BARNARDO'S (HEAD OFFICE)
Tanners Lane
Barkingside
ILFORD
IG6 1QG
Tel: 020 8550 8822
www.barnardos.org.uk

BARNARDO'S JIGSAW PROJECT
12 Church Hill
Walthamstow
LONDON
E17 3AG
Tel: 020 8521 0033

BARNARDO'S NEW FAMILIES PROJECT
54 Head Street
COLCHESTER
Essex

CO1 1PB
Tel: 01206 562438

**CATHOLIC CHILDREN'S
SOCIETY (ARUNDEL &
BRIGHTON, PORTSMOUTH &
BRIGHTON)**
49 Russell Hill Road
PURLEY
Surrey
CR8 2XB
Tel: 020 8668 2181
Email: info@cathchild.org
www.cathchild.org.uk

**CATHOLIC CHILDREN'S
SOCIETY (DIOCESE OF CLIFTON)**
58 Alma Road
Clifton
BRISTOL
BS8 2DJ
Tel: 0117 973 4253
Email: info@ccsclifton.org.uk

**CATHOLIC CHILDREN'S
SOCIETY (FAMILY MAKERS
GRAVESEND)**
Family Finders
28 Leith Park Road
GRAVESEND
DA12 1LW
Tel: 01474 352521

**CATHOLIC CHILDREN'S
SOCIETY (LITTLEHAMPTON)**
4 St Catherine's Road
LITTLEHAMPTON
West Sussex
BN17 5HS
Tel: 01903 715317

**CATHOLIC CHILDREN'S
SOCIETY (WINCHESTER)**
7 Bridge Street
WINCHESTER

SO23 8HN
Tel: 01962 842024

**CATHOLIC CHILDREN'S
SOCIETY(WESTMINSTER)
CRUSADE OF RESCUE**
73 St Charles's Square
LONDON
W10 6EJ
Tel: 020 8969 5305

CHILDLINK ADOPTION SOCIETY
10 Lion Yard
Tremadoc Road
LONDON
SW4 7NQ
Tel: 020 7501 1700

**THE CHILDREN'S SOCIETY
(HEAD OFFICE)**
Public Enquiry Unit
Edward Rudolf House
69 – 89 Margery Street
LONDON
WC1X 0JL
Tel: 020 7841 4436
www.the-childrens-society.org.uk

CORAM FAMILY
49 Mecklenburgh Square
LONDON
WC1N 2QA
Tel: 020 7520 0300
Email: reception@coram.org.uk
www.coram.org.uk

**EXETER DIOCESE BOARD FOR
CHRISTIAN CARE (FAMILIES
FOR CHILDREN)**
Glenn House
96 Old Tiverton Road
EXETER
EX4 6LD
Tel: 01392 278875

**INDEPENDENT ADOPTION
SERVICE**
121 – 123 Camberwell Road
LONDON
SE5 0HB
Tel: 020 7703 1088
Email: admin@i-a-s.org.uk
www.independentadoptionservice.org.uk

NCH (CENTRAL OFFICE)
85 Highbury Park
LONDON
N5 1UD
Tel: 020 7704 7000
www.nch.org.uk

NCH
Resources Team
Weirhouse
93 Whitby Road
St Phillips
BRISTOL
B54 4AR
Tel: 0117 3005360

NCH
Adoption NCH South East
158 Crawley Road
Roffey
HORSHAM
West Sussex
RH12 4EU
Tel: 01403 225916

NCH
Office 3
The Stable
65 The High Street
NEWMARKET
Cambridgeshire
CB8 8NA
Tel: 01638 561303

**NORWOOD JEWISH ADOPTION
SOCIETY**
Broadway House

80 – 82 The Broadway
STANMORE
Middlesex
HA7 4HB
Tel: 020 8954 4555
Email: jackygordon@nwrw.rog
www.nwrw.org

**PARENTS AND CHILDREN
TOGETHER (PACT)**
7 Southern Court
South Street
READING
Berkshire
RG1 4QS
Tel: 0118 9387600
email: info@pactcharity.org

PARENTS FOR CHILDREN
41 Southgate Road
LONDON
N1 3JP
Tel: 020 7359 7530
Email: info@parentsforchildren.co.uk

**SOLDIERS' SAILORS' AIRMENS'
FAMILIES ASSOCIATION (SSAFA)
– FORCES HELP**
19 Queen Elizabeth Street
LONDON
SE1 2LP
Tel: 020 7403 8783
*Email: services-support@ssafa-forces-
help.org.uk*
www.ssafa.org.uk

**ST FRANCIS' CHILDREN'S
SOCIETY**
Collis House
48 Newport Road
Woolstone
MILTON KEYNES
MK15 0AA
Tel: 01908 572700
Email: enquiries@sfcs.org.uk
www.sfcs.org.uk

CYMRU

BAAF CYMRU
7 Cleeve House
Lambourne Crescent
CARDIFF
CF14 5GJ
Tel: 029 2076 1155
Fax: 029 2074 7934
Email: cymru@baaf.org.uk

and at

19 Bedford Street
RHYL
Denbighshire
LL18 1SY
Tel: 01745 336336
Fax: 01745 362362
Email: cymru.rhyl@baaf.org.uk

LOCAL AUTHORITY AGENCIES

ANGLESEY COUNTY COUNCIL, ISLE OF
Social Services Department
County Offices
LLANGEFNI
LL77 7TW
Tel: 01248 752733

BLAENAU GWENT COUNTY BOROUGH COUNCIL
Social Services Department
107 – 110 Worcester Street
BRYNMAWR
NP23 4JP
Tel: 01495 313803

BRIDGEND COUNTY BOROUGH COUNCIL
Personal Services Directorate
Council Offices, Sunnyside
BRIDGEND
CF31 4AR
Tel: 01656 642200
Email: jonesja@bridgend.gov.uk

CAERPHILLY COUNTY BOROUGH COUNCIL
Social Services Department
Family Placement Team
6 Piccadilly Square
CAERPHILLY
CF83 1PB
Tel: 029 20880090

CITY AND COUNTY OF CARDIFF
Children's Services
Trowbridge Centre
Greenway Road
CARDIFF
CF3 8QS
Tel: 029 2077 4600

CARMARTHENSHIRE COUNTY COUNCIL
Social Services Department
3 Spilman Street
CARMARTHEN
SA31 1LE
Tel: 01267 234567 Ext 2903

CEREDIGION COUNTY COUNCIL
Social Services Department
Headquarters
Min Aeron, Vicarage Hill
Aberaeron
CEREDIGION
SA46 0DY
Tel: 01545 572630

CONWY COUNTY BOROUGH COUNCIL
Family Placement Team
Civic Offices Annexe
Abergele Road
COLWYN BAY
Conwy
LL29 8AR
Tel: 01492 514871
Email: gwilym.roberts@conwy.gov.uk

DENBIGHSHIRE COUNTY COUNCIL
Social Services Department
Cefndy Children's Resource Centre
Cefndy Road
RHYL
Denbighshire
LL18 2HG
Tel: 01745 332468
Email: micksams@denbighshire.gov.uk
www.denbighshire.gov.uk

FLINTSHIRE COUNTY COUNCIL
Social Services Department
County Offices, Civic Centre
Wepre Drive
CONNAHS QUAY
Flintshire

CH5 4HB
Tel: 01352 701000

GWYNEDD COUNCIL
Social Services Department
Penrallt
CAERNARFON
Gwynedd
LL55 1BN
Tel: 01286 682646

ISLE OF ANGLESEY COUNTY COUNCIL
See ANGLESEY COUNTY COUNCIL

MERTHYR TYDFIL COUNTY BOROUGH COUNCIL
Social Services Department
Taf Fechan Buildings
Castle Street
MERTHYR TYDFIL
CF47 8BG
Tel: 01685 724500

MONMOUTHSHIRE COUNTY COUNCIL
Monmouthshire Social Services
Newbridge House
Baker Street
ABERGAVENNY
Monmouthshire
NP7 5HY
Tel: 01873 735900

NEATH PORT TALBOT COUNTY BOROUGH COUNCIL
The Laurels
87 Lewis Road
NEATH
SA11 1DJ
Tel: 01639 765400

NEWPORT COUNTY BOROUGH COUNCIL
Children & Family Services
Adoption & Fostering
Corn Exchange, High Street

NEWPORT
NP20 1RN
Tel: 01633 246571

PEMBROKESHIRE COUNTY COUCIL
Family Placement Team
The Elms
Golden Hill Road
PEMBROKE
SA71 4QB
Tel: 01646 683747
Email:
david.halse@pembrokeshire.gov.uk

POWYS COUNTY COUNCIL
Social Services Department
Third Floor, The Gwalia
Ithon Road
LLANDRINDOD WELLS
Powys
LD1 6AA
Tel: 01597 827331
Email: chrisdavies@powys.gov.uk

RHONDDA CYNON TAFF COUNTY BOROUGH COUNCIL
Maes-y-Coed
Looked After Children's Services and
Education Services
Maes-y-Coed
Lanelay Terrace
Pontypridd
RHONDDA CYNON TAFF
CF37 1ER
Tel: 01443 490710

SWANSEA COUNTY COUNCIL
Social Services Department
Cockett House
Cockett Road
COCKETT
Swansea
SA2 0FJ
Tel: 01792 522900

TOERFAEN COUNTY BOROUGH COUNCIL
Social Services Department
County Hall
CWMBRAN
Torfaen
NP44 2WN
Tel: 01633 648536

VALE OF GLAMORGAN COUNCIL
Children & Family Services
Haydock House
1 Holton Road
BARRY
CF63 4HA
Tel: 01446 725202

WREXHAM COUNTY BOROUGH COUNCIL
Personal Services Department
3 – 9 Grosvenor Road
Guild Hall
WREXHAM
LL11 1DB
Tel: 01978 291422

VOLUNTARY AGENCIES

BARNARDO'S
Derwen Family Placement Services
11 – 15 Colombus Walk
Atlantic Wharf
CARDIFF
CF10 5BZ
Tel: 029 2043 6200
www.barnardos.org.uk

CATHOLIC CHILDREN & FAMILY CARE (WALES)
Bishop Brown House, Durham Street
Grangetown
CARDIFF
CF1 7PB
Tel: 029 2066 7007
Email: ccfcs@netscapeonline.co.uk

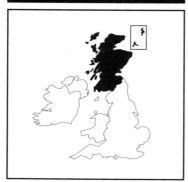

BAAF SCOTLAND
40 Shandwick Place
EDINBURGH
EH2 4RT
Tel: 0131 220 4749
Fax: 0131 226 3778
Email: scotland@baaf.org.uk

West of Scotland Family Placement Consortium
274 Bath Street
GLASGOW
G2 4JR
Tel: 0141 332 9880
Fax: 0141 332 8393
Email:
west.scotland@baaf.org.uk

LOCAL AUTHORITY AGENCIES

ABERDEEN CITY COUNCIL
Social Work Department
4 Albyn Place
ABERDEEN
AB10 1YH
Tel: 01224 646491 Ext 127

ABERDEENSHIRE COUNCIL
Family Placement Team
Inverurie Day Centre
Port Road
INVERURIE
AB51 3SP
Tel: 01467 629046

ANGUS COUNCIL
Social Work Department
Bruce House
Wellgate
ARBROATH
DD11 3TS
Tel: 01241 435096
Email: russellc@angus.gov.uk
www.angus.gov.uk

ARGYLL AND BUTE COUNCIL
Department of Housing & Social Work
Dalriada House
Lochnell Street
LOCHGILPHEAD
PA31 8ST
Tel: 01546 602177
Email: dougie.dunlop@argyll_bute.gov.uk

CLACKMANNANSHIRE COUNCIL
Social Work Department
Alloa Centre
8 Hillcrest Drive
ALLOA
FK10 1SB
Tel: 01259 225000
Email: rgoodwin@clacks.gov.uk

**COMHAIRLE NAN EILEAN SIAR
(WESTERN ISLES COUNCIL)**
Social Work Department
Council Offices
Rathad Shanndabhaig (Sandwick Road)
STEORNABHAGH (STORNOWAY)
Isle of Lewis
HS1 2BW
Tel: 01851 703773
Email: imacaulay@cne-siar.gov.uk

**DUMFRIES AND GALLOWAY
COUNCIL**
Social Work Department
2 – 6 Nith Street
DUMFRIES
DG1 2PW
Tel: 01387 249961

DUNDEE CITY COUNCIL
Social Work Department
Floor 7, Tayside House
28 Crichton Street
DUNDEE
DD1 3RN
Tel: 01382 434000
Email: jenni.tocher@dundeecity.gov.uk

EAST AYRSHIRE COUNCIL
Social Work Department
PO Box 13
Civic Centre, John Dickie Street
KILMARNOCK
KA1 1BY
Tel: 01563 576000

EAST DUNBARTONSHIRE COUNCIL
Social Work Department
2 – 4 West High Street
Kirkintilloch
GLASGOW
G66 1AD
Tel: 0141 775 9000

EAST LOTHIAN COUNCIL
Children and Family Resource Team

Sinclair McGill Buildings
Lodge Street
HADDINGTON
EH41 3DX
Tel: 01620 826600

EAST RENFREWSHIRE COUNCIL
Social Work Department
Lygates House, 224 Ayr Road
NEWTON MEARNS
East Renfrewshire
G77 6DR
Tel: 0141 577 3367

CITY OF EDINBURGH COUNCIL
Social Work Department
Springwell House, 1 Gorgie Road
EDINBURGH
EH11 3LA
Tel: 0131 313 3366

FALKIRK COUNCIL
Social Work Services
Brockville, Hope Street
FALKIRK
FK1 5RW
Tel: 01324 506400
Email: kathy.mccarroll@falkirk.gov.uk

FIFE COUNCIL
Family Placement Team
Rosyth Social Work Office
Park Road
ROSYTH
Fife
KY11 2JL
Tel: 01383 3133333

GLASGOW CITY COUNCIL
Families for Children
Centenary House, 100 Morrison Street
GLASGOW
G5 8LM
Tel: 0141 420 5555
Email: families.children@glasgow.gov.uk

HIGHLAND COUNCIL
Family Resource Centre
Limetree Avenue
INVERNESS
IV3 5RH
Tel: 01463 234120

INVERCLYDE COUNCIL
Social Work & Housing Services
195 Dalrymple Street
GREENOCK
PA15 1UN
Tel: 01475 714038
Email: lesley.watson@inverclyde.gov.uk
www.inverclyde.gov.uk

MIDLOTHIAN COUNCIL
Social Work Department
4 Clerk Street
LOANHEAD
Midlothian
EH20 9DR
Tel: 0131 271 3992
Email: edith_spencer@midlothian.gov.uk

MORAY COUNCIL
Social Work Department
29 – 31 Blackfriars Road
ELGIN
IV30 1TY
Tel: 01343 541669
Email:
dave.cameron@comm.moray.gov.uk

NORTH AYRSHIRE COUNCIL
Elliot House
Redburn Industrial Estate
Kilwinning Road
IRVINE
KA12 8TB
Tel: 01294 317771

NORTH LANARKSHIRE COUNCIL
Social Work Department HQ
Scott House, 73/77 Merry Street
MOTHERWELL

ML1 1JE
Tel: 01698 332045

ORKNEY ISLANDS COUNCIL
Social Work Department
Children and Families Team
Laing Street
KIRKWALL
Orkney
KW15 1NW
Tel: 01856 870193

PERTH AND KINROSS COUNCIL
Education & Children's Services
Pullar House, 35 Kinnoull Street
PERTH
PH1 59D
Tel: 01738 476200
Email: aparker@pkc.co.uk

RENFREWSHIRE COUNCIL
Social Work Department
North Building
4th Floor, Cotton Street
PAISLEY
PA1 1BU
Tel: 0141 842 5158

SCOTTISH BORDERS COUNCIL
Family Placement Team
1 Chapel Street
SELKIRK
TD7 4LB
Tel: 01750 21926
Email: mablackie@scotbord.com

SHETLAND ISLANDS COUNCIL
Social Work Department
91 – 93 St Olaf Street
LERWICK
Shetland
ZE1 0ES
Tel: 01595 744444
Email:
stephen.morgan@sil.shetland.gov.uk

SOUTH AYRSHIRE COUNCIL
Social Work Office
12 Main Street
PRESTWICK
KA9 1NX
Tel: 01292 470099
Email:
irene-callaghan@south.ayrshire.gov.uk

SOUTH LANARKSHIRE COUNCIL
Social Work Department
Adoption & Fostering
9 High Patrick Street
HAMILTON
ML3 7ES
Tel: 01698 454895
Email:
amanda.lyndsey@southlanarkshire.gov.uk

STIRLING COUNCIL
Social Work Department
Drummond House, Wellgreen Place
STIRLING
FK8 2ET
Tel: 01786 441177

WEST DUNBARTONSHIRE COUNCIL
Social Work Department
Council Offices
Garshake Road
DUNBARTON
G82 3PU
Tel: 01389 737739
Email: jim.watson@west-dunbarton.gov.uk

WEST LOTHIAN COUNCIL
Resources Team
Lomond House
Beveridge Square
LIVINGSTON
EH54 6QF
Tel: 01506 775960
www.webwest

WESTERN ISLES COUNCIL
See COMHAIRLE NAN EILEAN SIAR

VOLUNTARY AGENCIES

BARNARDO'S FAMILY PLACEMENT SERVICES
6 Torphichen Street
EDINBURGH
EH3 8JQ
Tel: 0131 228 41212

FAMILY CARE
21 Castle Street
EDINBURGH
EH2 3DN
Tel: 0131 225 6441
Email: birthlink@charity.vfree.com

ST ANDREW'S CHILDREN'S SOCIETY
Gillis Centre
113 Whitehouse Loan
EDINBURGH
EH9 1BB
Tel: 0131 452 8248
Email: Info@standrews-children.org.uk
www.standrews-children.org.uk

ST MARGARET CHILDREN & FAMILY CARE SOCIETY
274 Bath Street
GLASGOW
G2 4JR
Tel: 0141 332 8371

SCOTTISH ADOPTION ASSOCIATION
2 Commercial Street
Leith
EDINBURGH
EH6 6JA
Tel: 0131 553 5060

NORTHERN IRELAND

BAAF does not have an office in Northern Ireland. Enquiries should be directed to:

BAAF Southern Region
200 Union Street
LONDON
SE1 0LX
Tel: 020 7593 2041

Note: Adoption and Fostering Units are located in Health and Social Services Trusts which are divided into four regional Boards.

EHSSB COMMUNITY TRUSTS

DOWN LISBURN HEALTH & SOCIAL SERVICES TRUST
Warren Resource Centre
61 Woodland Park
LISBURN
BT28 1LQ
Tel: 028 92 607528

ULSTER COMMUNITY & HOSPITALS TRUST
Homefinding Team
Dunlop Units 57 & 58
4 Balloo Drive
BANGOR
BT19 7QY
Tel: 028 91 270672

NORTH & WEST BELFAST HEALTH AND SOCIAL SERVICES TRUST
Glendinning House
6 Murray Street
BELFAST
BT1 6DP
Tel: 028 90 327156

SOUTH & EAST BELFAST HEALTH & SOCIAL SERVICES TRUST
33 Wellington Park
BELFAST
BT9 6DL
Tel: 028 90 321313

NHSSB COMMUNITY TRUSTS

HOMEFIRST HEALTH & SOCIAL SERVICES TRUST
Children's Services Directorate
Pinewood Offices
101 Fry's Road

BALLYMENA
BT43 7EN
Tel: 028 25 658531

CAUSEWAY HEALTH & SOCIAL SERVICES TRUST
Family Placement Team
Riverside House, 28 Port Stewart Road
COLERAINE
BT52 1RN
Tel: 028 70 358158

WHSSB COMMUNITY TRUSTS

FOYLE HEALTH & SOCIAL SERVICES TRUST
Shantallow Health Centre
Racecourse Road
LONDONDERRY
BT48 8NL
Tel: 028 71 351350

SPERRIN LAKELAND HEALTH & SOCIAL SERVICES TRUST
Fostering and Adoption Team
Community Services Building
Block B
Tyrone and Fermanagh Hospital
OMAGH
BT79 0NS
Tel: 028 82 255033

SHSSB COMMUNITY TRUSTS

ARMAGH & DUNGANNON HEALTH & SOCIAL SERVICES TRUST
Family Placement Service
The Bungalow
Drumglass Lodge
20 Coalisland Road
DUNGANNON

BT71 6LA
Tel: 028 87 752033

CRAIGAVON & BANBRIDGE COMMUNITY HEALTH & SOCIAL SERVICES TRUST
Child and Family Care Office
2 Old Lurgan Road
PORTADOWN
BT63 5SQ
Tel: 028 3833 3747 / 028 38 333747

NEWRY & MOURNE HEALTH & SOCIAL SERVICES TRUST
5 Downshire Place
Downshire Road
NEWRY
BT34 1DZ
Tel: 028 30 260505
Email:
trust.headquarters@dhh.n-i.nhs.uk

VOLUNTARY AGENCIES

CHURCH OF IRELAND ADOPTION SOCIETY
Church of Ireland House
61 – 67 Donegal Street
BELFAST
BT1 2QH
Tel: 028 90 233885 / 028 90 233885 ext 227
Email: bsr@ireland.anglican.org
www.cofiadopt.org.uk

FAMILY CARE SOCIETY (NORTHERN IRELAND)
511 Ormeau Road
BELFAST
BT7 3GS
Tel: 028 9069 1133
Email: email@family-care-society.co.uk

BAAF and other useful organisations

British Association for Adoption and Fostering (BAAF)

BAAF is the leading UK-wide organisation for all those working in the adoption, fostering and childcare fields. BAAF's work includes giving advice and information to members of the public on aspects of adoption, fostering and childcare issues; publishing a wide range of books, training packs and leaflets as well as a quarterly journal on adoption, fostering and childcare issues; providing training and consultancy services to social workers and other professionals to help them improve the quality of medical, legal and social work services to children and families; giving evidence to government committees on subjects concerning children and families; responding to consultative documents on changes in legislation and regulations affecting children in or at risk of coming into care; and helping to find new families for children through *Be My Parent*.

Almost all local authority and voluntary adoption agencies are members of BAAF. You can join BAAF as an individual member; contact the Membership Officer for details of benefits and fees. Telephone 020 7593 2023 or visit www.baaf.org.uk for more information. BAAF is a registered charity.

Be My Parent

Every month, between 300 and 400 children waiting for new permanent families are featured in *Be My Parent*, the UK-wide family-finding newspaper published by BAAF. Subscribers to *Be My Parent* include approved adopters, those waiting to be approved and those who have only just begun to think about adopting or permanently fostering. Children of all ages and with a wide range of needs from all over the country are featured, and therefore *Be My Parent* seeks as wide a readership as possible. Many hundreds of families (married couples and single people) have adopted after first having seen their child's photograph and read their profile in *Be My Parent*. It is easy to subscribe and have the newspaper sent directly to you – just telephone the number below. If you see children in *Be My Parent* whom you would like to become part of your family, one telephone call to our staff will begin the process that could lead to you becoming approved to adopt that child.

Be My Parent is at

BAAF
Skyline House
200 Union Street
London SE1 0LX
Tel: 020 7593 2060/1/2
Email: bmp@baaf.org.uk

| Scottish Resource Network

The Scottish Resource Network is a child placement service run by BAAF in Scotland. The West of Scotland Consortium facilitates the placement of children across local authority boundaries in Scotland. Information about the Scottish Resource Network and West of Scotland Consortium can be obtained from BAAF Scotland (see below).

| BAAF Offices

More information about BAAF can be obtained from:

Head Office	**BAAF Scotland**	**BAAF Cymru**
Skyline House	40 Shandwick Place	7 Cleeve House
200 Union Street	Edinburgh EH2 4RT	Lambourne Crescent
London SE1 0LX		Cardiff CF14 5GP
Tel: 020 7593 2000	*Tel: 0131 220 4749*	*Tel: 029 2076 1155*
Fax: 020 7593 2001	*Fax: 0131 226 3778*	*Fax: 029 2074 7934*
Email:	*Email:*	*Email:*
mail@baaf.org.uk	*scotland@baaf.org.uk*	*cymru@baaf.org.uk*

A full list of BAAF's offices is provided in Chapter 9.

The Adoption Register

This is a database of waiting approved adopters and children. It is run by a voluntary adoption agency on behalf of the Department of Health. It will operate initially in England and Wales, although it may eventually extend to Scotland. It will be operational by April 2002.

Local authority adoption agencies will be expected to refer all approved adopters and all children for whom adoption is the plan immediately the decision is made. However, active linking of families and children will take place after local links have been explored. This should take a maximum of six months for a child, ie. three months to explore families on the local authority's own list and a further three months to explore local consortium families. Families can be held locally for six months, with an additional three months for a possible consortium link. Your agreement must be given before you are referred to the Register.

Voluntary adoption agencies will be encouraged to refer families for active linking immediately after approval.

Organisations for parents

Adoption UK
Supporting adoptive families before, during and after adoption

Adoption UK is a parent-to-parent network of over 3,500 established and potential adoptive families. It welcomes enquiries from prospective adopters; offers local support groups all over the UK; publishes a wide range of useful leaflets and *Adoption Today* – a bi-monthly magazine written by and for adopters, which also features children waiting for adoption. Current membership rate on request – or visit their website.

Adoption UK
Manor Farm, Appletree Road

Chipping Warden, Banbury
Oxfordshire OX17 1LH
Tel: 0870 7700 450
Helpline: 0870 7700 450
E-mail: admin@adoptionuk.org.uk
www.adoptionuk.org.uk.

AFAA (The Association for Families who have Adopted from Abroad)

A network of families who have adopted from abroad and offer support and advice to others considering the same.

AFAA
Carlton Lodge
Woodhead Wortley
Sheffield S35 7DA
Membership and Subscriptions Tel: 01142 885 845
Adviceline: 01707 878793
www.afaa.org.uk

Contact a Family

Contact a Family is a national charity for any parent or professional involved with or caring for a child with disabilities. Through a network of mutual support and self-help groups, Contact a Family brings together families whose children have disabilities, and offers advice and information to parents who wish to start a support group.

Contact a Family
209 – 211 City Road
London EC1V 1JN
Tel: 020 7608 8700
Fax: 020 7608 8701
Email: info@cafamily.org.uk
Minicom: 020 7608 8702
www.cafamily.org.uk

Post and after adoption centres

There are many well established after adoption services now that provide a service for adoptive families, adopted people and birth parents whose children were adopted. Many of them offer advice and counselling, in person, but also on the telephone or by correspondence, for individuals and families. Some also organise events which focus on matters related to adoption, and provide the opportunity for people to meet in common interest groups.

Post-Adoption Centre
5 Torriano Mews, Torriano Avenue
London NW5 2RZ
Tel: 020 7284 0555
Email: advice@postadoptioncentre.org.uk

After Adoption
12 – 14 Chapel Street, Salford
Manchester M3 7NN
(covers Northwest and Northeast England)
Tel: 0161 839 4930
Email: administration@afteradoption.org.uk

After Adoption Newcastle
Cale Cross House, 156 Pilgrim Street
Newcastle NE1 6TF
Helpline: 0845 601 0168
Email: northeast@afteradoption.org.uk

After Adoption Yorkshire
31 Moor Road, Headingley
Leeds LSG 4BG
Tel: 0113 2302100
Fax: 0113 278 6487
Email: aay@dialstart.net

After Adoption Working in Wales
7 Neville Street, Riverside
Cardiff CF11 6LP
Helpline: 029 2066831
Email: Southwales@afteradoption.org.uk

West Midlands Post Adoption Service (WMPAS)
4th Floor, Smithfield House
Digbeth
Birmingham B5 6BF
Tel: 0121 666 6014
Email: wmpasemail@aol.com

Family Care Birthlink
21 Castle Street
Edinburgh EH2 3DN
Tel: 0131 225 6441
Email: birthlink@charity.vfree.com

Barnardo's Scottish Adoption Advice Service
16 Sandyford Place
Glasgow G3 7NB
Tel: 0141 339 0772
Email: saas@barnardos.org.uk

SWAN (South West Adoption Network)
Leinster House, Leinster Avenue
Knowle
Bristol BS4 1NL
Helpline: 0845 601 2459
Email: helpline@swan-adoption.org.uk

Local authorities may also provide help and support. In Scotland, they have a duty to help adoptive families, adopted children and birth families. They sometimes use the help of voluntary agencies for this.

Fostering

Fostering Network
(formerly NFCA)

Fostering Network
87 Blackfriars Road
London SE1 8HA
Tel: 020 7620 6400
Fax: 020 7620 6401
Email: info@fostering.net
www.fostering.net

Fostering Network
(Scotland)

Fostering Network
Ingram House, 2nd Floor
227 Ingram Street
Glasgow G1 1DA
Tel: 0141 204 1400
Fax: 0141 204 6588
Email:nfca@fostercare-scotland.org.uk
www.fostercare-scotland.org.uk

Other organisations

ISSUE

ISSUE is the national self-help organisation which provides
information, support and representation to people with fertility
difficulties and those who work with them.

Membership   £20 per year
                  £7.50 low income

ISSUE
114 Lichfield Street
Walsall WS1 1SZ

Tel: 01922 722888
Fax: 01922 640 070
Email: webmaster@issue.co.uk
www.issue.co.uk

The National Organisation for Counselling Adoptees and their Parents (NORCAP)

NORCAP is a self-help support group for all parties to adoption. It offers advice for members on searching and a research service. It can play an intermediary role for those seeking renewed contact. NORCAP maintains a successful Contact Register and publishes a newsletter three times a year.

Initial membership £25.00 including entry on the Contact Register; annual subscription renewal £16 per year; entry on to the Contact Register without membership £10.

NORCAP
112 Church Road
Wheatley
Oxon OX33 1LU
Tel: 01865 875000

Overseas Adoption Helpline

The **Overseas Adoption Helpline** offers advice and information about current policy and practice in relation to overseas adoption and the legal requirements of the UK and "sending" countries. It produces a useful information pack with information about particular countries, and also runs group events.

Overseas Adoption Helpline
64 – 66 High Street
Barnet
Herts EN5 55J
Tel: 0870 5168 742

Useful books and leaflets

| Books for adults

Talking about Adoption to your Adopted child
PRUE CHENNELLS AND MARJORIE MORRISON
A guide to the whys, whens, and hows of telling adopted
children about their origins.
BAAF 1998

Adopters on Adoption: Reflections on parenthood and children
DAVID HOWE
In this absorbing collection of personal stories, adoptive
parents whose children are now young adults describe the
importance and distinctiveness of adoptive parenting.
BAAF 1996

Whatever Happened to Adam? Stories about disabled children who were adopted or fostered
HEDI ARGENT
This remarkable book tells the stories of 20 young people with
disabilities and the families who chose to care for them.
Following their life journeys from joining their new families,
through childhood and adolescence and into preparation for
adulthood, it reveals the tremendous rewards of adopting or
fostering a disabled child.
BAAF 1998

First Steps in Parenting the Child who Hurts: Tiddlers and toddlers (2nd edition)
CAROLINE ARCHER
This book offers practical, sensitive guidance from an adoptive
parent through the areas of separation, loss and trauma in early
childhood which will encourage confidence in other adoptive
parents and foster carers and thereby enable enjoyment in
parenting young children.
Jessica Kingsley Publishers for Adoption UK 1999

Next Steps in Parenting the Child who Hurts: Tykes and teens
CAROLINE ARCHER

Follows on from the *First Steps* book and shows how love can be expressed towards the older adopted child, despite persistent and often extreme tests of that love. Includes a review of specific sensitive situations that commonly arise and suggests some solutions.
Jessica Kingsley Publishers for Adoption UK 1999

The Adoption Experience: Families who give children a second chance
ANN MORRIS

Actual adopters tell it like it is on every part of the adoption process from the exciting moment of first deciding to adopt to feelings about children seeking a reunion with their natural families or simply leaving home.
Jessica Kingsley Publishers for Adoption UK in association with the *Daily Telegraph* 1999

Books for use with children

Nutmeg Gets Adopted
JUDITH FOXON

. Nutmeg and his siblings are young squirrels who go into foster care when their mother finds she cannot keep them safe, and they are then adopted. Beautifully illustrated in full colour, this story will help children in similar situations explore and understand some of the very painful memories they will have of their early life. Includes practice guidelines suggesting how the book can be used with children of different ages.
BAAF 2001

Chester and Daisy Move on
ANGELA LIDSTER

A picture book for 4 – 10-year-olds which tells the story of two bear cubs that have to leave their family. Work pages are

provided to help children parallel or contrast their own experiences and feelings.
BAAF 1995

Bruce's Multimedia Story

Bruce is a "spaniel sort of dog" who has to leave his mum and dad, stay in kennels with his brothers and sisters, and eventually go to live with a new family.

This electronic version of *Bruce's Story* is designed to capitalise on children's natural interest in computer-based activities and introduces animation, sound effects, music, speech and interactivity. The aim is to make the whole experience more interesting and more fun for the children and hence, more productive for worker and child together.
Information Plus 1998

My Life and Me

JEAN CAMIS

This colourful, comprehensive and durable life story work book can be used flexibly with any child growing up away from their birth family, including children adopted from abroad. Includes guidelines to completing the various sections for anyone doing direct work with children.
BAAF 2001

BAAF Children's book series

A unique series of books for use with children separated from their birth parents. The stories are simply told and attractively illustrated in full colour. Worksheets at the back of each book will help children to compare and contrast their own experiences with those of the characters in the story.

Living with a New Family: Nadia and Rashid's story (1997)

Nadia is 10 and Rashid seven. When their father died some years ago, their birth mother, Pat, found it hard to look after them. So Nadia and Rashid went to live with Jenny, a foster carer, and then with their new parents, Ayesha and Azeez.

Belonging doesn't Mean Forgetting: Nathan's story (1997)
Nathan is a four-year old African-Caribbean boy and has just
started school. His birth mother, Rose, found it hard to be a
good mum and wanted someone else to look after him. Nathan
went to live with foster carers Tom and Delores. And then
with Marlene, her daughter Sophie, Grannie and Aunty Bea.

Hoping for the Best: Jack's story (1997)
Jack is an eight-year-old white boy. His birth mum, Maria,
couldn't look after him because she was unhappy and unwell.
Jack went to live with Peter and Sarah. At first he was happy
but then started to feel sad and mixed up. Peter and Sarah did
not think they could be the right mum and dad for him and
Jack had to leave.

Feeling Safe: Tina's story (1998)
Tina wasn't safe at home and now lives with Molly who is her
foster carer. Tina had to move after she told a teacher about
how her Dad's touches made her feel bad. She is not sure
whether she will ever be able to live with her family again but
feels safe with her foster family.

Joining Together: Jo's story (1998)
Tomorrow will be a big day for eight-year-old Jo. She is going
to court with her mum, stepfather and baby brother to be
adopted. Jo knows that although Dave isn't her birth father he
wants to help look after her for the rest of her life.

Waiting for the Right Home: Daniel's story (2001)
When Daniel's parents split up, he moves to live with his mum
and her new partner. But it doesn't work out. His dad's flat is
too small for the two of them so Daniel goes to live with foster
carers Jeff and Vivien. Will Daniel stay there? Or will he go to
live with his father and grannie? This is a story about living
with foster carers for a short while before going home.

| Advice Notes

BAAF's popular leaflet series called Advice Notes contains essential information about key areas in adoption and fostering.

Adoption – some questions answered
Basic information about adoption. Explains the adoption process including the legal issues and the rights of birth parents.

Foster care – some questions answered
Basic information about fostering. Explains different types of foster care, the relationship with the local authority and legal aspects.

Meeting children's needs through adoption and fostering
Information for people considering adopting or fostering a child with special needs.

Private fostering
Aimed at those considering private fostering in England and Wales, this leaflet explains what private fostering involves, and provides guidance of what prospective carers need to know.

Stepchildren and adoption
Information for birth parents and step-parents on stepfamilies, the advantages or not of adoption, and obtaining further advice. Two editions available: one for England and Wales and one covering Scotland.

| Other useful BAAF | leaflets

Understanding the assessment process: information for prospective adopters and carers
This is a very useful leaflet for anyone thinking about applying to offer a permanent home to a child. It gives a broad

overview of what will be involved including references, social work interviews, reports and decision-making.

Intercountry adoption – information and Guidance
Information on adopting a child from overseas, including procedures, legislation, and where to obtain advice and further information.

Form ICA
Intercountry adoption form (medical report and development assessment of child) which, when ordered individually, comes with two copies of Form AH (previously called Form Adult 1) for the prospective adoptive parents.

All the publications listed (with the exception of *Adoption Today*) are available from BAAF publications, tel. 020 7593 2072. A free catalogue listing all our titles is also available, or you can find them listed on www.baaf.org.uk.

Periodicals listing children who need new families

Be My Parent
A UK-wide monthly newspaper for adopters and permanent foster carers who may or may not be approved. It contains features on adoption and fostering and profiles of children across the UK who need new permanent families. Subscription details available; tel. 020 7593 2060/1/2.

Children in Scotland
As part of the Scottish Resource Network, BAAF Scotland produces a bi-monthly newsletter of children awaiting placement in Scotland. This is distributed to local authorities and voluntary adoption agencies and is available to approved adopters and long-term foster carers.

Adoption Today

Adoption Today is a bi-monthly journal published by Adoption UK and is available on subscription. It keeps members in touch with one another, profiles children needing new permanent families, and gives information on general developments in the field of adoption.

Glossary of terms

Below is a glossary of certain terms that appear in the book. In cases where there is a difference between England and Wales and Scotland, this is shown.

Accommodated/ Accommodation

England and Wales

Under section 20 of the Children Act 1989, the local authority is required to "provide accommodation" for children "in need" in certain circumstances. The local authority does not acquire parental responsibility (see below) merely by accommodating a child and the arrangements for the child must normally be agreed with the parent(s), who, subject to certain circumstances, are entitled to remove the children from local authority accommodation at any time.

Scotland

Under section 25 of the Children (Scotland) Act 1995, the local authority must "provide accommodation" for the children in certain circumstances and may also do so in other situations. Normally, the accommodation is provided by agreement with the parent(s), they can then remove the child at any time in most circumstances. Parental responsibilities remain with the parent(s). A child accommodated under section 25 is a "looked after child" (see below).

Adoption allowance

Adoption agencies can, in certain circumstances, pay a regular allowance to enable an adoption to go ahead which could not otherwise do so for financial reasons. The allowance must be agreed by the agency before the Adoption Order is made.

| Adoption panel

Adoption agencies (local authorities or voluntary adoption societies) are required to set up an adoption panel which must consider and make recommendations on children for whom adoption is the plan, on prospective adopters and on matches between prospective adopters and children.

| Care Order

Applies only to England and Wales. A child who is subject to a Care Order is described as being "in care". A Care Order gives the local authority parental responsibility for the child but does not deprive the parent(s) of this. Nevertheless, the local authority may limit the extent to which parents may exercise their parental responsibility and may over-ride parental wishes in the interests of the child's welfare.

| Children's guardian

England and Wales
A person appointed by the court to safeguard a child's interests in court proceedings (formerly called a guardian *ad litem*). Local authorities are required to establish panels of people to act as children's guardians (and reporting officers – see below) in care proceedings and in adoption proceedings. Their duties are set out in court rules and include presenting a report to the court.

| Consortium

A group of usually not more than 6 – 8 local adoption agencies, often both local authorities and voluntary adoption agencies, who share details of waiting families and children in order to try and make speedy local placements for children.

| Contact/Contact Order

England and Wales

Contact may be used to mean visits, including residential visits or other form of direct face-to-face contact between a child and another individual, or it may mean indirect ways of keeping in touch (eg. letters or telephone calls including letters sent via a third party). A Contact Order under the Children Act 1989 is an order requiring the person with whom the child lives to permit the child to have contact (direct or indirect) with the person named in the order.

Scotland

As in England and Wales, contact can mean direct or indirect contact or access. It covers private arrangements (eg. in divorce, etc), it also covers a public law situation when a child is "looked after" by a local authority. When a child is on a supervision requirement (see above) under the Children's Hearing system, the hearing regulates contact.

| Curator *ad litem*

Similar to children's guardian in England and Wales (see above).

| Freeing Order/freeing for adoption

England and Wales

A Freeing Order under the Adoption Act 1976 ends parents' parental responsibility and transfers parental responsibility to the adoption agency. The purpose of this is to allow any issue regarding parental consent to adoption to be resolved before the child is placed with prospective adopters. In certain circumstances the "former parent" may ask the court to revoke the order if the child is not placed with prospective adopters after one year.

Scotland

A Freeing Order under the Adoption (Scotland) Act 1978 has the same effect as above. It is an optional court process by a local authority before an application for adoption.

| Fostering/foster care

In this book this term is used for those cases where a child is placed with a foster carer approved by the local authority and/or placed directly by a voluntary organisation. These placements are governed by the Foster Placement (Children) Regulations 1991 in England and Wales and by the Fostering of Children (Scotland) Regulations 1996 in Scotland. "Short-term", "long-term" and "permanent" foster care and "respite care" may mean different things to different people – they are not legally defined terms.

| Guardian

A guardian is a person who has been formally appointed as a child's guardian after the death of one or both parents. The appointment may be made in writing by a parent or by a court.

| Looked after

England and Wales
This term includes both children "in care" and accommodated children. Local authorities have certain duties towards all looked after children and their parents, which are set out in Part III of the Children Act 1989. These include the duty to safeguard and promote the child's welfare and the duty to consult with children and parents before taking decisions.

Scotland
This term covers all children for whom the local authority has responsibilities under section 17 of the Children (Scotland) Act 1995. It replaces the term "in care". It is wider than and different from the English and Welsh definition. It includes children who remain at home as well as those placed away from home.

| Open adoption

This term may be used very loosely and can mean anything from an adoption where a child continues to have frequent face-to-face contact with members of his or her birth family to an adoption where there is some degree of "openness", eg. the birth family and adopters meeting each other once. People using the term should be asked to define what they mean!

| Parental responsibility

England and Wales

This is defined in the Children Act 1989 as 'all the rights, duties, powers and responsibilities which by law a parent has in relation to a child and his property'. When a child is born to married parents, they will both share parental responsibility for him or her, and this parental responsibility can never be lost except on the making of an Adoption Order. A father who is not married to the child's mother does not automatically have parental responsibility but may acquire it either by formal agreement with the mother or by court order. Confusingly the term "parents" when used in the Children Act includes both parents, whether or not the father has parental responsibility, but in the Adoption Act 1976, "parent" means only parents who have parental responsibility.

Parental responsibilities and rights – Scotland

These are what parents have for their children and are defined in sections 1 and 2 of the Children (Scotland) Act 1995. All mothers have them automatically; fathers only if married to the mother at conception or later. However, fathers can get them by formal agreement with the mother or by a court order.

Anyone can go to court for an order about parental responsibilities and rights under section 11 of the Children (Scotland) Act 1995. Residence Orders (see below) and Contact Orders (see above) are examples. The court can also take away responsibilities and rights under this section.

Parents or others with responsibilities and rights can only lose them by a court order: an Adoption Order, Parental Responsibilities Order (see below), or an order under section 11.

In relation to a father who is not married to the mother, the father can obtain these rights through an agreement under the Children (Scotland) Act 1995.

Parental Responsibilities Order

Scotland
This section removes all parental responsibility from the parent(s) (except the right to consent (or not) to adoption) and gives them to the local authority. It is granted under section 86 of the Children (Scotland) Act 1995.

Reporting officer

A member of the panel of children's guardians/curators *ad litem* and reporting officers, appointed by the court for adoption proceedings. His or her specific task is to ensure that the agreement of a parent or guardian to an Adoption Order if given is given freely and with full understanding of what is involved and to witness the agreement.

Residence Order

England and Wales
An order under the Children Act 1989 settling the arrangements as to the person/s with whom the child is to live. Where a Residence Order is made in favour of someone who does not already have parental responsibility for the child (eg. a relative or foster carer), that person will acquire parental responsibilities subject to certain restrictions (eg. they will not be able to consent to the child's adoption). Parental responsibility given in connection with a Residence Order will only last as long as the Residence Order. A Residence Order normally only lasts until the child's 16th birthday.

Scotland
This is one of the orders possible under section 11 of the Children (Scotland) Act 1995. It regulates with whom the child lives. If the

person with the Residence Order did not have any parental responsibilities and rights before, the order gives those as well.

Residence Order allowance

England and Wales

Local authorities have a power to contribute to the cost of a child's maintenance when the child is living with somebody under a Residence Order provided he or she is not living with a parent or step-parent. A financial contribution under this power is normally referred to as a Residence Order allowance.

Scotland

Local authorities have the power to pay an allowance to a person who has care of a child and who is not a parent or a foster carer. The person does not have to have a Residence Order.

Schedule 2 report

England and Wales

Under the court rules for adoption proceedings, a report has to be submitted to the court covering the details that are set out in Schedule 2 to the Adoption Rules 1984. In the case of an adoption which has been arranged by an adoption agency, or an application to free a child for adoption, this report is the responsibility of the placement agency. In cases where the adoption was not arranged by an adoption agency (eg., step-parents or intercountry adoption), the local authority prepares the report.

Section 23 or section 22 reports

Scotland

Reports to the court are under section 23 in agency adoptions and section 22 in non-agency cases, eg. step-parents, of the Adoption (Scotland) Act 1978. The Rules of Court give guidance about what should be in the reports.

| **Supervision requirements**

Scotland

These are the orders made by the Children's Hearing for any child needing compulsory measures of supervision. Children may be victims of abuse or neglect, have other problems and/or have committed crimes. All children on supervision requirements are "looked after" by the local authority, even if they live at home. Supervision requirements do not give parental responsibilities and rights to local authorities.